BASICS
FASHION DESIGN

A PRACTICAL GUIDE TO SUSTAINABLE FASHION

Fairchild Books
An imprint of Bloomsbury Publishing Plc

50 Bedford Square
London
WC1B 3DP
UK

1385 Broadway
New York
NY 10018
USA

www.bloomsbury.com

Bloomsbury is a registered trademark of Bloomsbury Publishing Plc

First published 2014

British Library Cataloguing-in-Publication Data

A catalogue record for this book is available from the British Library.

ISBN: PB: 978-2-940496-14-3
       ePDF: 978-2-940447-64-0

Library of Congress Cataloging-in-Publication Data

Gwilt, Alison.
  A practical guide to sustainable fashion / Alison Gwilt.
    pages cm
  Includes bibliographical references and index.
  ISBN 978-2-940496-14-3 (paperback : alkaline paper) -- ISBN 978-2-940447-64-0 (ePDF)
1. Clothing trade--Environmental aspects. 2. Clothing trade--Moral and ethical aspects.
3. Fashion design--Environmental aspects. 4. Fashion design--Moral and ethical aspects.
5. Sustainability. 6. Sustainable design. I. Title.
  TT497.G95 2014
  746.9'2--dc23

                    2013029983

Design by StudioInk
Printed and bound in China

**Cover illustration and 0.1 |
Biomimicry project by
Stefanie Nieuwenhuyse.**

Fashion designer, illustrator
and textile designer, Stefanie
Nieuwenhuyse used discarded
pieces of plywood and laser-
cutting techniques to produce a
range of garments for her Masters
project (see pages 44–45).

A Practical Guide to Sustainable Fashion **foregrounds the idea that fashion designers have the opportunity to bring sustainability into the design and production process, in contrast to some corners of the fashion industry where sustainability is regarded as an obstruction to good design. However, many fashion designers currently feel confused about how to do this, and from a designer's perspective it can be difficult to know where to begin to find help, assistance and guidance in developing sustainable fashion. This book presents an inspiring yet practical model for the fashion designer to reference and use within the studio environment.**

Instructor and student resources to accompany this book are available at: http://tinyurl.com/qhxkjnf

Please type the URL into your browser and follow the instructions to the online resources. If you have any problems, please contact: instructor-resources@bloomsbury.com

0.2 | REtrose label by Emma Rees.

Through her label, REtrose, UK designer Emma Rees uses digital print, sustainable fabrics and discarded materials and garments for new womenswear collections.

0.2

A Practical Guide to Sustainable Fashion suggests that it is imperative for the fashion designer to understand the key phases within the life cycle of a garment and that, armed with this knowledge, it becomes possible to improve a garment's environmental and ethical credentials. Drawing on examples from both well-known fashion brands and companies, and innovative, emerging designers, the book explores a variety of ways in which designers can bring sustainablility into the fashion design process, from focusing on designing garments for disassembly and recycling at the point of disposal, to developing garments that are energy-efficient during the use phase.

While this book will guide and steer you to explore new ways of designing and producing garments, it also proposes that producers should reflect on the system of fashion itself. The fashion industry should ideally be moving away from a model that relies solely on achieving economic success from the manufacture of products, to considering a model of practice that incorporates, for example, product–service combinations including leasing, repair and alteration services, and take-back schemes. This will require those working in the fashion industry to explore new, more sustainable approaches to the design and production process.

Featuring practical exercises and insightful interviews with contemporary designers from around the world, *A Practical Guide to Sustainable Fashion* will inspire and support you to embed sustainability in your approach to designing and producing fashion.

Chapter 1 begins with a reflection on the current fashion design and production process, and introduces the key issues surrounding sustainability and the fashion industry today. This chapter looks at how designers have engaged with sustainable design ideas since the late 1960s, and discusses the opportunities that designers have to reduce the negative environmental and social impacts associated with a garment's life cycle.

Chapter 2 introduces the key phases and activities in the life cycle of a garment, along with an approach for assessing and evaluating the environmental and social impacts of a new fashion garment during the design phase. This chapter also explores how sustainable design strategies are currently being used within the fashion industry to reduce the negative impacts associated with garment production.

The following five chapters explore in turn each key phase of the garment life cycle: design, production, distribution, use and end-of-life. Each chapter explores a variety of ways in which sustainable design strategies can be integrated into the design and production process. The chapters include several 'Spotlight on' features looking at selected approaches, which are supported by visual examples of best practice from dress history and contemporary fashion labels by designers, students and researchers. There are also practical exercises to enable you to experiment with the approaches presented in the book.

0.3

0.3 and 0.4 | 'Sustainable Earth Sweater' by Iniy Sanchez.

Dutch designer, Iniy Sanchez produces knitwear pieces that are made from one continuous thread, which can be unravelled and reused.

0.4

This chapter introduces the key issues associated with the current fashion design and production process. It also discusses key developments in sustainable fashion and looks at the role of the fashion designer in making improvements.

As the critical link in the chain of design and production, fashion designers have both the ability and the opportunity to develop products that can lessen our impact on the environment while addressing social and ethical concerns.

'I can honestly say that I did not start as an eco brand; I just became one as soon as I was exposed to how much we were throwing out and consuming.'

Orsola de Castro, co-founder of From Somewhere

1.1 | From Somewhere 'Fluff Cardigan', AW12.

From Somewhere is a successful fashion label that is built on recycling pre-consumer textile waste to form beautiful high-fashion garments. The designers use production offcuts, ends of rolls and other surplus materials.

The fashion industry is now made up of a variety of market levels, ranging from haute couture and bespoke tailoring to mass-market brands and online shopping. The characteristics of the garments and the scale of production vary according to the market level, but broadly speaking the design and production process involves a common set of stages that occur within all market levels of the industry. This process, which is also known as the 'supply chain', includes five distinct stages: design, sample-making, selection, manufacturing and distribution.

Each stage in the process involves a set of activities that range from sourcing and selecting materials and processes, and designing the different 'looks' within the collection (the design stage), to distributing garments from the place of manufacturing to the retailers or customers (the distribution stage). The time dedicated to the manufacturing stage often differs according to the scale of production and the manufacturing method used. For example, a smaller fashion label can produce selected samples relatively quickly compared with a larger company. This may be partly due to the fact that manufacturing is taking place offshore and may be related to the need to approve a factory sample range, for quality purposes, before manufacturing takes place.

The role of the fashion designer

Many people employed within the fashion industry make an important contribution in the process of creation; the fashion system employs designers, buyers, pattern makers, machinists, knitters, textile designers, finishers and dyers, production managers and so on, and each brings specialist skills and knowledge. In most cases, the designer will be expected to lead the development of the collection from the design stage through to the sample-making stage, and will often be accountable for key decisions during the process.

1.2 | Activities in the fashion supply chain.

The key stages and activities in the supply chain are illustrated here. The way in which companies engage with their supply chain model varies between different brands, but the phases within the supply chain typically remain constant.

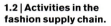

Rethinking fashion design

1.2

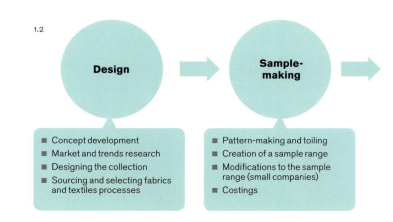

Design

- Concept development
- Market and trends research
- Designing the collection
- Sourcing and selecting fabrics and textiles processes

Sample-making

- Pattern-making and toiling
- Creation of a sample range
- Modifications to the sample range (small companies)
- Costings

Market levels

Haute couture
Haute couture is considered to be the highest and most specialized level of fashion, showing two seasonal collections a year. The garments are made to measure by a haute couture house, such as Chanel or Dior.

Luxury brand
Luxury brands, such as Louis Vuitton, Bottega Veneta and Fendi, use high-profile advertising to promote products including perfumes, accessories and a range of luxury goods alongside ready-to-wear (RTW) collections. Designers may be brought in to develop the RTW collections.

Designer/RTW
Designer/RTW companies range from small independent labels, such as Jonathan Saunders, to more established designers such as Dries Van Noten, and also include the RTW collections from haute couture houses such as Chanel. The garments are produced in standard sizes, although the labels retain an air of exclusivity since the garments embody the designer's individual design aesthetic.

High-street brand
High-street fashion companies or mass-market brands produce and buy in large volumes of collections that may be sold in their own stores. The lead time from sketch to finished product can be a matter of weeks, and new collections will arrive in-store at frequent intervals during the season, sometimes each fortnight, as with retailers H&M and Topshop.

Online/home shopping
Provides access to a wide range of garments, sometimes not available in-store, and delivers directly to the home. Online shopping is currently booming since it provides convenience and allows smaller, niche or independent labels to reach the consumer directly.

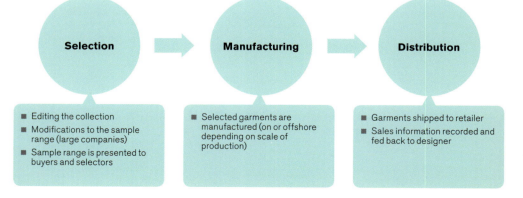

Selection
- Editing the collection
- Modifications to the sample range (large companies)
- Sample range is presented to buyers and selectors

Manufacturing
- Selected garments are manufactured (on or offshore depending on scale of production)

Distribution
- Garments shipped to retailer
- Sales information recorded and fed back to designer

The production, use and disposal of fashion clothing have a wide range of impacts. In general terms, these can be considered from an environmental and a social perspective. As a society, the obsession for consuming fashion goods has seen an enormous growth in mass-produced fashion, in particular 'fast fashion' that focuses on bringing runway trends to the high street in the quickest possible time.

The issues outlined in figure 1.3, which take into account the stages in the supply chain along with consumer-based phases, represent a number of environmental and ethical concerns that are often associated with fast-fashion clothing, but they also represent the multiplicity of problems that the fashion industry in general is facing. The fashion industry is made up of a global network of suppliers, producers and retailers, and so the battle to make improvements involves liaising with a multitude of stakeholders, working under different laws and legislation.

Fast fashion and JIT technology

'Just-in-time' (JIT) technology makes use of new production technologies that allow a garment to be manufactured up to 30 per cent or 40 per cent more quickly than when using conventional processes, without building up unnecessary stock. Although approaches may vary, a producer can use technology-enabled facilities to handle specific functions. For example, rather than outsourcing work to manufacturers, fast-fashion producer and retailer Zara handles its own supply chain and has built a number of factories that use robots to handle specialist processes. The aim is to speed up the time it takes to move from a sketch to a finished garment.

1.3 | Social and environmental impacts along the clothing supply chain.

(From the report *Fashioning Sustainability*, Forum for the Future.)

1.3

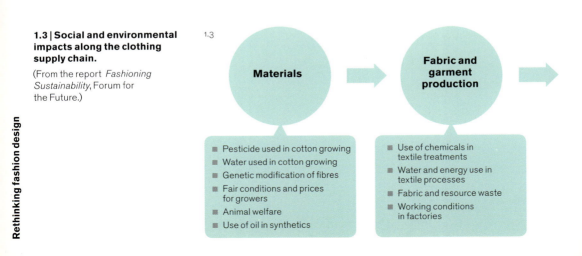

Materials

Fabric and garment production

- Pesticide used in cotton growing
- Water used in cotton growing
- Genetic modification of fibres
- Fair conditions and prices for growers
- Animal welfare
- Use of oil in synthetics

- Use of chemicals in textile treatments
- Water and energy use in textile processes
- Fabric and resource waste
- Working conditions in factories

1.4

1.5

1.4 and 1.5 | *The Cotton Film: Dirty White Gold*. Directed by Leah Borromeo and produced by Dartmouth Films.

The Cotton Film: Dirty White Gold is a documentary feature film that traces the supply chain of cotton from seed to shop. Traditional cotton farming relies heavily on pesticides and uses vast amounts of water. Meanwhile, the life of the cotton-picker is hard, often involving poor pay and long hours.

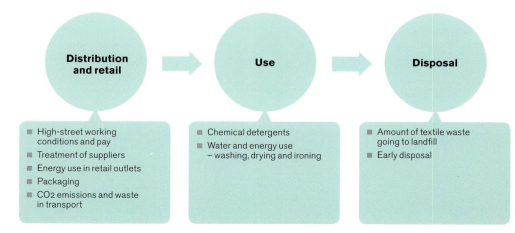

Distribution and retail → **Use** → **Disposal**

- High-street working conditions and pay
- Treatment of suppliers
- Energy use in retail outlets
- Packaging
- CO_2 emissions and waste in transport

- Chemical detergents
- Water and energy use – washing, drying and ironing

- Amount of textile waste going to landfill
- Early disposal

1.6

Consumption of fashion

Once a garment has been purchased, the owner becomes responsible for its care and maintenance. Called the 'use phase', this stage involves the garment going through many different activities including wearing, washing, drying, storing, and extends to repairing, adaption and alteration. Each person develops a clothing care and maintenance routine based on personal patterns of use, which may be different from those used by other people. However, a number of studies have shown that most of the environmental impacts associated with clothing are created during the use phase, largely due to the laundering process, which uses energy, water and chemical detergents.

Although a large amount of textile waste in particular can be attributed to wasteful manufacturing methods, waste can also be attributed to poor consumer care routines, early disposal of functioning garments and a lack of repair and alteration skills. Garments are often discarded too quickly before possibilities for repair or alteration are considered. Moreover, there are many different recycling options for unwanted garments, helping to minimize the amount of textile waste reaching landfill or incineration. It is important that designers understand how garments are used and discarded so they can begin to develop new garments that will help bring about improved patterns of use.

Rethinking fashion design

1.6 | Marks & Spencer (M&S) 'Shwopping' campaign.

Working with the UK charity Oxfam, M&S encouraged the public to donate clothing for reuse, resale or remanufacture through their 'Shwopping' campaign.

1.7 | The Local Wisdom project.

Originated by Dr Kate Fletcher, Reader in Sustainable Fashion at the London College of Fashion, the Local Wisdom project explores the reasons behind why people keep specific items of clothing.

Where do garments go after disposal?

According to the report *Well Dressed? The Present and Future Sustainability of Clothing and Textiles in the United Kingdom* (University of Cambridge Institute for Manufacturing, 2006), approximately 2.35 million tonnes of textile waste are generated in the UK over a year. Of this, 74 per cent is sent to landfill, while 26 per cent is shared equally between material recovery and incineration. This statistic reveals that a huge amount of clothing and textile waste is either being dumped in landfill sites or incinerated rather than recycled. All materials have some form of value, whether they are reused in a garment or recycled to become underlay.

Since UK consumers will on average contribute as much as 30kg of textile waste per capita to landfill, there appears to be an enormous opportunity to further encourage consumers to recycle unwanted clothes.

1.7

Among the many different market levels that the fashion industry now supports, there is a growing market for sustainable fashion. Although sustainable fashion may appear to be a relatively recent concept, initial concerns regarding design and the environment were raised in the 1960s. Since then, different approaches to reducing the impact of fashion on the environment and society have been taken. While the focus has often remained on selecting appropriate materials, the contemporary fashion industry is now embracing many different avenues alongside careful fabric selection.

1.8

1.8 | Edun SS12.

Established by Ali Hewson and Bono in 2005, Edun strives to build long-term relationships with suppliers, manufacturers and artisans in African communties to bring about positive change.

1960s–1970s

It was during the 1960s and 1970s, as environmentalists began to voice their concerns over the impact and devastation of a consumerist society, that an interest in finding more sustainable approaches to production and consumption began to emerge. By the 1970s a number of environmental groups, such as Friends of the Earth and Greenpeace, had begun to voice concerns about environmental degradation, and a responsible design movement emerged following the publication of Victor Papanek's seminal text, *Design for the Real World* (1971). Rachel Carson's book *Silent Spring* (1962) was pivotal in providing a critical account of the environmental damage caused by cotton growing and the textile manufacturing industry.

1980s–1990s

While music and film influenced fashion in the 1980s and spurred subculture groups to embrace vintage styles, a small number of designers began to explore eco-efficiency in product design. By the late 1980s, at a time of an overwhelming boom in the growth of designer goods, a small sector of environmentally concerned consumers had emerged. The Italian knitwear firm Benetton also began to produce a series of controversial advertising campaigns that provoked debates on topics such as racism, human rights and world hunger.

By the 1990s 'eco-design' was being championed by environmentally aware designers, while at the same time a growing market of socially and environmentally conscious consumers emerged, favouring brands with environmental credentials such as Birkenstock shoes. The fashion industry began to experiment with the concept of environmentalism and eco-fashion, with specialized collections from international high-street companies such as Esprit. However, even though organic cotton was appearing on the high streets, it did not fare well with the cost-conscious consumer.

Eco design

Eco or green design attempts to avoid the environmental impacts that are associated with a garment during its life cycle. The aim is to prevent, reduce or eliminate impacts that may pollute, destroy or reduce the planet's natural resources.

2000s

In recent years, following a move away from developing a green or eco product, there has been a repositioning towards the broader concept of design for sustainability. This acknowledges a holistic approach to sustainability that includes a consideration of social issues within a long-term product innovation strategy. The response from the fashion industry to these concerns can be seen in a number of highly visible case studies within the mass-market retail and outdoor/performance wear sectors.

Companies such as Marks and Spencer (UK), Patagonia (USA), Terra Plana (UK) and Nike (USA) are all implementing a number of sustainable strategies across areas of design and production. Outside the mass-market fashion and outdoor/performance wear sectors, UK high-fashion design labels such as Stella McCartney and Katharine Hamnett have continually responded positively to environmental and ethical ideals by using environmentally friendly materials and processes.

Sustainable design strategies

A sustainable design strategy is considered to be a framed approach that can be employed by a designer to help reduce specific environmental and/or social impacts associated with the production, use and disposal of a product.

Research relating to the use of sustainable strategies within design practice initially appeared within the context of industrial design, and over the last four or five years many of these strategies have been explored and adopted by fashion designers.

1.9 | 'Don't Buy this Jacket' advert from Patagonia, 2011.

Patagonia's Don't Buy This Jacket advert appeals to consumers to consider the environmental effect of their purchases. The US outdoor clothing company produces fleece garments manufactured from post-consumer waste such as plastic water bottles; the company also uses a closed-loop system of production in which unwanted polyester garments are recycled and reused for the manufacture of a fleece fibre for new product ranges.

1.9

DON'T BUY
THIS JACKET

It's Black Friday, the day in the year retail turns from red to black and starts to make real money. But Black Friday, and the culture of consumption it reflects, puts the economy of natural systems that support all life firmly in the red. We're now using the resources of one-and-a-half planets on our one and only planet.

Because Patagonia wants to be in business for a good long time – and leave a world inhabitable for our kids – we want to do the opposite of every other business today. We ask you to buy less and to reflect before you spend a dime on this jacket or anything else.

Environmental bankruptcy, as with corporate bankruptcy, can happen very slowly, then all of a sudden. This is what we face unless we slow down, then reverse the damage. We're running short on fresh water, topsoil, fisheries, wetlands – all our planet's natural systems and resources that support business, and life, including our own.

The environmental cost of everything we make is astonishing. Consider the R2® Jacket shown, one of our best sellers. To make it required 135 liters of

COMMON THREADS INITIATIVE

REDUCE
WE make useful gear that lasts a long time
YOU don't buy what you don't need

REPAIR
WE help you repair your Patagonia gear
YOU pledge to fix what's broken

REUSE
WE help find a home for Patagonia gear you no longer need
YOU sell or pass it on*

RECYCLE
WE will take back your Patagonia gear that is worn out
YOU pledge to keep your stuff out of the landfill and incinerator

REIMAGINE
TOGETHER we reimagine a world where we take only what nature can replace

water, enough to meet the daily needs (three glasses a day) of 45 people. Its journey from its origin as 60% recycled polyester to our Reno warehouse generated nearly 20 pounds of carbon dioxide, 24 times the weight of the finished product. This jacket left behind, on its way to Reno, two-thirds its weight in waste.

And this is a 60% recycled polyester jacket, knit and sewn to a high standard; it is exceptionally durable, so you won't have to replace it as often. And when it comes to the end of its useful life we'll take it back to recycle into a product of equal value. But, as is true of all the things we can make and you can buy, this jacket comes with an environmental cost higher than its price.

There is much to be done and plenty for us all to do. Don't buy what you don't need. Think twice before you buy anything. Go to patagonia.com/CommonThreads or scan the QR code below. Take the Common Threads Initiative pledge, and join us in the fifth "R," to reimagine a world where we take only what nature can replace.

patagonia®
patagonia.com

TAKE THE PLEDGE

* If you sell your used Patagonia product on eBay® and take the Common Threads Initiative pledge, we will co-list your product on patagonia.com for no additional charge.

Sustainable fashion today should consider three key areas: society (which should focus on social equity), the environment (which should focus on ecological stability) and the economy (which focuses on economic viability). The challenge for designers is to manage these three facets responsibly and embrace a holistic approach to sustainability.

This can begin by looking at the way that garments are produced and investigating avenues that can reduce and improve the environmental and social impacts associated with fashion. Although designers are becoming more aware of the environmental and ethical impacts connected to different fibres and fabrics, it is important to look for opportunities that go beyond a reliance on the selection of materials. Many exciting and creative opportunities can arise from establishing a better connection with other parts of the supply chain and the people within it.

Understanding life-cycle thinking

A key point to remember is that a garment has a life cycle that goes beyond the retail store. Traditionally, the fashion supply chain has been concerned with designing, manufacturing and distributing garments. But it is important to acknowledge that garments have a use phase and a disposal phase; and, as a designer, you may be able to influence the patterns of use during these two key phases of your garment's life cycle. From this perspective, the concept and speed of fashion can be challenged. For example, a garment can be complemented with a service system and kept for a lifetime, a jacket may be shared rather than owned, and a shirt may be safely recycled over and over again.

1.10

Rethinking fashion design

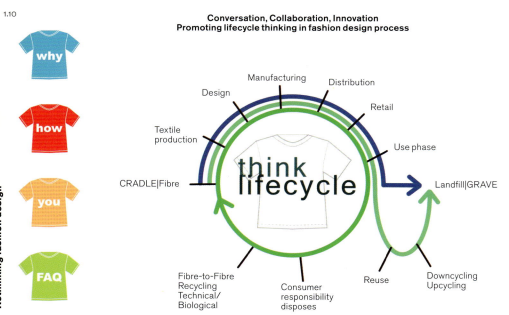

**Conversation, Collaboration, Innovation
Promoting lifecycle thinking in fashion design process**

1.11

1.10 | ThinkLifecycle CMS by Alice Payne.

Researcher Alice Payne is developing
ThinkLifecycle, a Content Management System
(CMS) for the fashion industry, which will provide
an online platform for sharing ideas and knowledge
across the staff within a company.

**1.11 | AW11 denim mix 'OMG' suit jacket
from Junky Styling.**

Junky Styling deconstructs and transforms existing,
unwanted clothing into new garments.Customers
can bring their own garments into the 'wardrobe
surgery' for revitalization.

Life cycle

The term 'life cycle' refers to the journey of a
product from the extraction of the raw fibre to
the point of its disposal.

The responsibility of the designer

As discussed earlier, the fashion designer is responsible for leading the development of a collection and will need to liaise with a wide range of people during the process. However, it should be remembered that designers must consider the principles of sustainable design in relation to their own particular situation and apply them appropriately and with conviction.

Fashion producers have frequently adopted a tokenistic approach to sustainability, but paying lip service to sustainability can have the adverse effect of weakening the credibility of the sustainable agenda. This 'greenwashing' has occurred in a number of retail markets and could also happen in mainstream fashion markets if sustainability issues are not convincingly addressed.

1.12

1.12 and 1.13 | People Tree AW12.

As a member of the World Fair Trade Organization, fair trade fashion pioneer and online garment retailer People Tree focuses on producing fashion clothing that aims to improve the lives and conditions of the farmers and producers who make their products.

1.13

Making improvements

A number of resources relating to sustainable fashion are now available, which provide information on materials and textiles techniques, production methods and consumer care routines (see, for example, the resources section at the end of this book). But as you become more aware of sustainable fabrics, fibres and textiles techniques, the real challenge will be to engage with sustainability while still meeting the range of aims and objectives outlined in your design brief. It can, however, be particularly difficult to know where to begin when designing sustainable garments; but at the design stage, it is possible to identify the potential impacts of a new garment in preparation for making improvements. To engage in this process, designers need to have a good understanding of the activities and phases of a garment's life cycle. This will be explored in the following chapter.

Greenwashing

A term used to describe the false or overexaggerated environmental claims of a company or product. It is often associated with advertising, promotion or marketing.

1.14   1.15

**1.14 and 1.15 |
Ada Zanditon AW11.**

Ada Zanditon's philosophy is to create desirable fashion using sustainable business practices, which includes sourcing ethical and environmentally friendly textiles, and producing the collections in London.

Katharine Hamnett

Since the 1980s, British designer Katharine Hamnett has engaged in activism through fashion as a means of encouraging society to take notice of critical issues affecting people and the environment. Hamnett is considered an ambassador in the fashion industry, and has been continuously campaigning for improved ethical and environmental production practices.

In 1983, Hamnett began to produce her slogan protest T-shirt, a product that became her signature item. Most famously, in a meeting with the then Prime Minister, Margaret Thatcher, in 1984, Hamnett protested against missile systems wearing the T-shirt '58% Don't Want Pershing'. In 1989, in her AW collection 'Clean Up or Die', Hamnett tried to persuade the fashion industry to reflect on the impacts of cotton farming on both the environment and the lives of the cotton-growing farmers. She has since continued her campaign work speaking out about issues associated with cotton production, and is an ardent promoter of the benefits of organic cotton.

In 2011, she relaunched her label Katharine E Hamnett, and she remains committed to the benefits of using organic cotton; her T-shirts are now produced in socially certified factories that house advanced dyeing and water treatment facilities.

To coincide with the UK's Climate Week in 2012, Hamnett collaborated with the Environmental Justice Foundation (EJF) to launch the 'Save the Future' organic cotton T-shirt. Sold through fashion retailer H&M, sales raised much-needed funds for EJF initiatives, but it is the message that is considered important. 'Save the future. There's been too much hot air, let's do something now', stated Hamnett in support of the campaign that intends to help some of the world's poorest people displaced by the impacts of environmental damage.

<www.katharinehamnett.com>

1.16

1.16 | 'Save the Future' T-shirt by Katharine Hamnett.

In 2012, Hamnett collaborated with the Environmental Justice Foundation (EJF) and fashion retailer H&M on the iconic 'Save the Future' slogan T-shirt.

1.17 | 'No More Fashion Victims' T-shirt by Katharine Hamnett.

Katharine Hamnett worked with development organization Helvetas and the Environmental Justice Foundation (EJF) to launch the 'No More Fashion Victims' T-shirt. The T-shirts were made from 100 per cent organic cotton from Mali.

Rethinking fashion design

1.17

Reflecting on sustainable fashion

Although there are now a growing number of sustainable fashion labels, there are also many different approaches to designing and producing sustainable garments. This exercise will encourage you to reflect on some of the ways in which designers are bringing sustainability into the fashion design and production process.

Your task is to use a variety of sources – including books, the Internet and magazine and journal articles – to find three sustainable fashion labels that are each using a different approach.

You must find a fashion label that is:

■ recycling or upcycling waste materials to make new clothes;

■ using organic or sustainable fabrics in the production of new fashion products;

■ producing garments designed to be kept for a long time.

Using visuals and text statements, create a mood board that reflects your findings. How is each label approaching design and production? Compare the differences between the labels. Which approach do you find interesting? Could you apply any of these approaches to your own design practice?

1.18 | The 'Tant Brun' jacket from Annika Matilda Wendelboe's Panache Collection, 2013.

Swedish designer Annika Matilda Wendelboe was one of the first designers to develop a fully recyclable fashion collection using Cradle to Cradle Certified fabrics. Garments such as the 'Tant Brun' jacket shown here can be either composted or recycled.

1.18

In this chapter, you will learn how to apply life cycle thinking to fashion design and production. The phases of a garment's life cycle are discussed, as is how to identify the potential environmental and social impacts of the design and production process. This chapter also introduces a range of sustainable design strategies and how they can be applied within fashion design. A number of resources are highlighted to help you conduct further research into this process.

'I think it's important to educate one's self, to try to provide a high-quality product for the consumer and not to lose any of the desirability, and yet also to try to be more responsible in the way that you think and the way you source your materials.'
Stella McCartney

2.1 | Limited edition garment by From Somewhere and Speedo, 2010.

Created from unsold stock and surplus pieces of the Speedo LZR Racer suit, UK fashion label From Somewhere collaborated with Speedo to produce a limited range of garments.

The life cycle of a fashion garment can generally be broken down into five key phases: design, production, distribution, use and end-of-life. Applying a life cycle approach to the fashion design process requires thinking through all the stages in the life cycle of a garment and considering the environmental and social impacts of your design decisions. This process will allow you to evaluate and assess the sustainability credentials of your designs, and provide you with a starting point for making improvements.

2.2 | The life cycle of a fashion garment.

The stages in the life cycle of a garment, and the activities over which the fashion designer can have some influence.

2.2

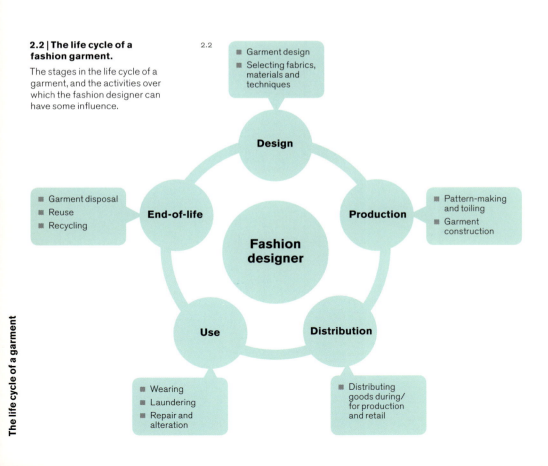

- Garment design
- Selecting fabrics, materials and techniques

Design

- Garment disposal
- Reuse
- Recycling

End-of-life

Fashion designer

Production

- Pattern-making and toiling
- Garment construction

Use

Distribution

- Wearing
- Laundering
- Repair and alteration

- Distributing goods during/ for production and retail

The process for making improvements

In order to begin making improvements, you need to consider a number of stages.

The first step is to map the life cycle of the product to be developed, which is best done at the start of the design process. This may entail focusing on one single garment or grouping together garment types that you know share similarities.

The second step is to identify the key issues by conducting an assessment of the environmental and social impacts of your product. The third step is to evaluate the results and pick out the significant issues to be addressed. The fourth step is to engage with the relevant sustainable strategies that can help to reduce or eliminate the issues without creating negative impacts elsewhere in the garment's life cycle.

2.3 | Design for Change project by Clara Vuletich, 2012.

Designer and researcher Clara Vuletich reuses denim waste that has been gathered from three points within the supply chain for a new range of accessories.

2.3

Information about the environmental and social impacts of fashion garments can be revealed by 'mapping' the activities in the life cycle of a garment. It is important to establish some boundaries at the start of this process. For example, you may decide to begin your assessment with the sourcing of materials rather than beginning from the extraction of raw fibres. However, you will need to question your suppliers and be confident that they can supply you with accurate information.

The following is a guide to the phases and activities that a garment will go through during its life cycle. It is important to note that the activities assigned to a phase may shift and move depending upon the circumstances of individual companies (see 'Market levels in fashion' on page 13).

2.4

Design

The design phase in the life cycle of a garment can include activities such as market and trends research, developing a concept and designing the collection. But it is important to remember that the design process also includes activities such as identifying and sourcing fabrics, trimmings and finishing processes.

Production

Once the fabrics have been selected and the design concepts determined, the designer, often in collaboration with specialists such as pattern-cutters and machinists, will develop the sample range. This may involve using techniques such as flat pattern-making or draping on the stand. The way in which the final garment is manufactured is determined by the approaches applied during pattern-making and sample-making, so it is critical to explore these two activities.

The life cycle of a garment

Distribution

It is important to remember that distribution issues can stretch across the entire life cycle of a garment. Distribution networks are required to transport materials for the design and production process (sample-making, toiling and pattern-making) as well as to transport the final garments to the retailers or directly to the consumer's home. It is also important to consider your labelling and packaging needs at this stage.

Use

When considering the life cycle of a garment, the use phase is typically highlighted as an area for concern, mostly due to the impacts associated with laundering (see Chapter 6). In order to make improvements across the whole life cycle, it is important that designers have an understanding of how garments are used, and why and how they are discarded.

End-of-life

As discussed in Chapter 1, textile waste is most often discarded into landfill or incinerated. However, a number of approaches can be used to delay this or divert garments away from landfill, such as recycling garments and engaging in closed-loop systems of production.

2.4 | 'New York Messenger' tote from the Quantum collection by Gunas.

Luxury accessories brand Gunas produces handbags that are sweatshop-free and eco-friendly.

Identifying the impacts

Once the life cycle has been mapped, the next step is to identify not only the impacts of the garment during its manufacture, but also the continuing impacts that occur during its use and disposal. As you think through the phases in the life cycle of your garment, you will need to record the 'inputs', for example the fabrics, trimmings, textiles processes, manufacturing and distribution methods, while also identifying the potential 'outputs' of your decisions.

2.7 | The impacts asscociated with each phase in the life cycle of a garment.

2.5

2.6

The roadmap of two garments' life cycle

In 2009, Australian fashion label Gorman worked with the Brotherhood of St Laurence to map the journey of two natural fibre garments so that the environmental and social impacts associated with fashion products could be better understood. Using a visual 'roadmap', the study revealed the impacts of a garment as it went through the key phases of design and production within the Gorman supply chain, beginning with design before moving to material production and garment manufacture, and then to retail and finally, disposal. The project involved interviewing company representatives, suppliers and industry associations and experts. You can visit the website and develop a map of your product.

Visit <http://tfia.assets1.blockshome.com/assets/events/69UPldISTRkbehf/bsl-travelling-textiles-garment-prm-report.pdf>

2.5 and 2.6 | Organic jersey tank tops from Gorman.

The life cycle of a garment

2.7

Inputs:
- What materials and supplies do you intend to use?
- What are they made from?
- What textile processes will you use?
- Do these processes require any resources?

Outputs:
- What outputs arise from textile treatments such as dyeing and printing?
- What outputs arise from raw material production processes?
- Can you see outputs related to the design of your garment?

Inputs:
- What happens to the garment at the end of its life?
- What services are required during the disposal phase?

Outputs:
- What impacts arise from the process of managing the waste material?
- Can the materials be reused or recycled?
- What will happen if the garment is placed in landfill or incinerated?
- Is there any impact on human health?

Inputs:
- Who makes your supplies and garments?
- Where are garments assembled?
- What resources are needed for production?

Outputs:
- What happens to the textile waste from your production?
- Will any other waste be created during production?
- Will there be any impact on the health and lives of people involved in production?

Design

End-of-life

Fashion designer

Production

Use

Distribution

Inputs:
- What services are required during the use phase?
- What is your preferred laundering process?
- How frequently does the garment need laundering?
- What is needed to maintain the garment?

Outputs:
- What outputs arise from your preferred laundering method?
- Is energy used for ironing or tumble-drying?
- Are chemicals used in dry-cleaning processes?
- Is there any impact on human health?

Inputs:
- What distance do your goods (pre- and post-production) have to travel?
- How are goods transported?
- What are your packaging needs?
- Do products need to be stored at any point?

Outputs:
- What is the energy and resource consumption associated with your transportation?
- How is packaging waste managed?

After you have identified the impacts connected to the activities in your garment's life cycle, the next step is to assess the information you have gathered. This will allow you to identify the key issues associated with your design.

2.8

The life cycle assessment model

A range of tools and models have been developed to help design and production teams measure the negative environmental impacts of their garments. The method most commonly used in industry to assess the life cycle impact of garments is the life cycle assessment (LCA) model. An assessment typically explores energy and water use, waste and emissions of pollutants across the life cycle stages (although commonly it does not measure social or ethical impacts). The results are then quantified into a unit of measure per material or resource; these have usually been determined in relation to the guidelines and codes of practice established by the International Organization for Standardization. The results of the LCA are often shown using either a matrix or a spider or wheel diagram.

This type of assessment is commonly called a 'cradle-to-grave' approach. The 'cradle-to-cradle' approach, which aims to return materials safely back into the environment or into a closed-loop system of production, can be analysed using an LCA with the additional consideration of end-of-life strategies.

The life cycle of denim jeans

A good introduction to the information that can be revealed through an assessment is demonstrated in a study of the life cycle of denim jeans. A number of different studies have been conducted, all of which tend to highlight a common set of issues, particularly the extensive transportation of garment components between countries during manufacture, and the excessive amounts of water used in the cultivation of cotton during textile treatments and processes, and in laundering. Visit the Levis Strauss & Co website to find out what the life cycle of a pair of jeans looks like.

2.8 | 'Beth' women's jeans by Nurmi.
Finnish label Nurmi makes its production processes transparent to the consumer.

The life cycle of a garment

A simple assessment model

While industry tools are useful for measuring and comparing different materials and processes, designers need to consider sustainability as an integral part of the fashion design process and seek alternative strategies for designing and making clothes at the concept or research stage. At the early stages of the design process, the designer can evaluate a garment's life cycle using a simple evaluation tool, which can be handled manually or by using computer software. The tool may, for example, use a scale system ranging between 1 and 10 to measure impacts, the results then being translated into a visual spider or wheel diagram that highlights the problems to be addressed. Once the key environmental and social impacts have been identified, the next step is to look for ways to make improvements.

Industry tools and models

The EcoMetrics™ calculator
The EcoMetrics™ online calculator is an industry tool designed to measure the environmental impacts of different textiles and processes.
<www.colour-connections.com/EcoMetrics/>

The Nike Considered Index
Nike developed its software-based Environmental Apparel Design Tool to reduce the environmental footprint of its clothing and footwear. Using a numerical scoring system based on information entered, the final scores are placed in a category that ranges from 'Good' to 'Needs improvement'.
< www.nikebiz.com/crreport/content/environment/4-1-0-overview.php?cat=overview>

The Higg Index
This enables designers and companies to measure and evaluate the environmental impacts associated within various stages of a product's life cycle, for example, water use and quality, energy and greenhouse gases, waste, chemicals and toxicity.
<www.apparelcoalition.org/higgindex/>

2.9

Design

End-of-life

Production

Use

Distribution

Good OK Poor Bad

2.9 | Rating the impacts of a fashion garment.

There are many assessments tools available through the Internet, but you can use a template such as the one shown here, which will help you rate the impacts of your garment from good to bad.

As discussed in Chapter 1, sustainable design strategies focus on a specific approach to making improvements in the design, production, use and/or disposal phases of a product's life cycle. Engaging with a strategy involves meeting focused aims and objectives.

In addition, a strategy can be applied at one phase in the life cycle of a product or may extend across several phases. For example, the strategy of minimizing waste can be engaged across the entire life cycle of a garment if the design and production teams look for ways by which to minimize the waste of resources (materials, water, energy, and so on) at the outset of the design stage, during the manufacturing processes and during the disposal phase. Alternatively, a strategy may focus on making improvements in one specific phase; the strategy 'design for disassembly', for example, concentrates on creating a product that can be easily disassembled at the end of its useful life so that the material components can be reused or recycled.

2.10

2.10 | Nicole Bridger AW12.

Vancouver-based designer Nicole Bridger uses sustainable materials, including organic cottons and Global Organic Textile Standard-certified wool, and produces 90 per cent of the collection in Vancouver, with fair trade producers manufacturing a small number of items.

The life cycle of a garment

2.11

2.12

2.11 | Upcycled sari scarf with kantha stitch, from House of Wandering Silk.

The fair trade organization House of Wandering Silk, based in India, produces unique silk and cotton scarves and throws by upcycling vintage saris. Handcrafted by local artisans, layers of saris are sewn together using a traditional kantha stitch.

2.12 | Childrenswear by Kallio.

Based in New York, Kallio is a childrenswear brand that reuses men's business shirts for children's clothing and accessories.

How do sustainable design strategies work?

Many sustainable design strategies focus on making environmental improvements, which is an outcome of the extensive work that has been conducted within the area of eco- or green design. However, designers should also be concerned with the balance between social and ethical issues and economic needs, so strategies that aim to make improvements in these areas must be considered to be equally as important. The sustainable strategies that can be applied in a garment's design and production generally intend to meet one or more of the following principles:

- Minimizing the consumption of resources
- Choosing low-impact processes and resources
- Improving production techniques
- Improving distribution systems
- Reducing the impacts created during use
- Improving the garment's lifetime
- Improving the use of end-of-life systems

2.13

2.13 | Martina Spetlova SS13.

Martina Spetlova graduated from the Central Saint Martins MA course in 2010 and brings a patchwork approach to her use of recycled materials. Here, Spetlova intricately weaves together recycled materials to form high-fashion pieces that are both colourful and bold.

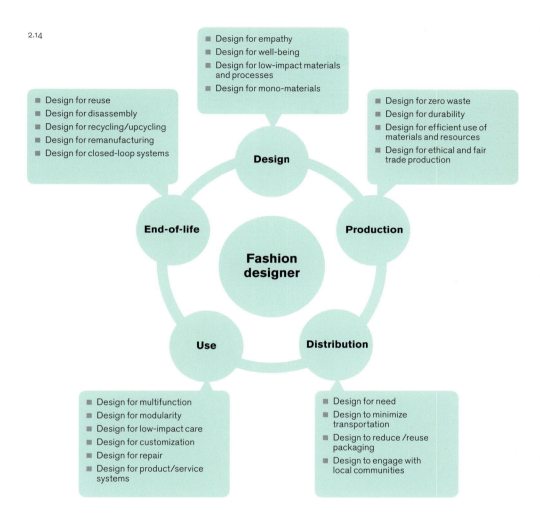

2.14

- Design for empathy
- Design for well-being
- Design for low-impact materials and processes
- Design for mono-materials

- Design for reuse
- Design for disassembly
- Design for recycling/upcycling
- Design for remanufacturing
- Design for closed-loop systems

- Design for zero waste
- Design for durability
- Design for efficient use of materials and resources
- Design for ethical and fair trade production

Design

End-of-life

Production

Fashion designer

Use

Distribution

- Design for multifunction
- Design for modularity
- Design for low-impact care
- Design for customization
- Design for repair
- Design for product/service systems

- Design for need
- Design to minimize transportation
- Design to reduce /reuse packaging
- Design to engage with local communities

2.14 | Using sustainable design strategies.

This model (developed by the author) shows the life cycle phases of a garment aligned with appropriate sustainable design strategies. The strategies mapped here are those already in use in the fashion industry, or are emerging from trials executed in experimental projects or research. The following chapters will explore a number of these strategies in more detail.

Using sustainable design strategies

Once you have evaluated your assessment and identified the key issues to be addressed, you can begin to select appropriate sustainable design strategies that will help to minimize or eliminate the negative impacts. To begin with, it may be useful to experiment with a single strategy to see how you can respond to a set aim or goal. This will not only introduce you to the creative potentials and opportunities of engaging with sustainability, but can also be a good way of seeing how sustainable design strategies can alter your perception of how you design and make garments.

However, for an ongoing engagement with sustainability, you will need to see sustainable strategies in relation to life cycle thinking. A key facet of life cycle thinking is to consider the consequences of decisions that we make, and to be mindful that improvements made at one stage in the life cycle of a garment should not negatively impact on another stage. It is important, then, that the burden should not be shifted elsewhere. So while you plot out the possible improvements that may result from engaging with a particular strategy, try also to look for any unwanted consequences.
An advantage of conducting this type of predictive exercise is that you may reveal potential improvements to explore through ongoing development. This means that you can be continually working towards making further improvements.

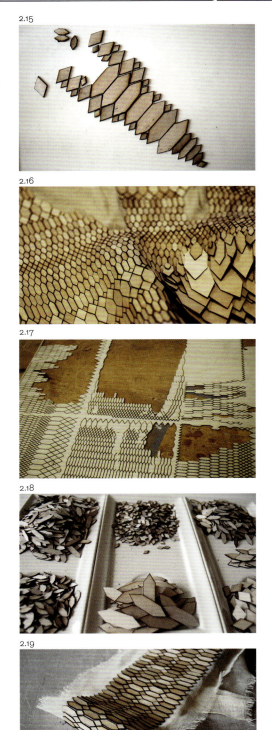

2.15

2.16

2.17

2.18

2.19

The life cycle of a garment

2.20

2.21

2.15–2.21 | Process shots from Stefanie Niewenhuyse's Biomimicry project.

Using discarded pieces of plywood donated by biowaste company InCrops Enterprise Hub, Stefanie Niewenhuyse developed an innovative concept for laser-cut textiles, which formed the foundation for a range of garments produced for her Masters project.

2.22 | Garments from Lu Flux's 'Everything but the Kitchen Sink' collection, AW12.

Fashion designer Lu Flux produces luxurious garments, incorporating complex knitting, pleating and antiquated patchworking techniques. Lu was awarded the Innovation Award in conjunction with the Ethical Fashion Forum celebrating her inventive and exciting designs in the world of sustainable fashion.

2.22

Stella McCartney

Stella McCartney is recognized as one of the most socially aware figures in the fashion industry. After joining Chloé as Creative Director in 1997, McCartney launched her own label in 2001. With 23 international stores and a worldwide network of wholesale accounts, McCartney's label has grown into a business that includes kidswear, fragrance, eyewear, lingerie and a collaboration with Adidas, alongside ready-to-wear pieces and accessories.

McCartney is known for never using leather, fur or exotic skins in her collections or collaborations. Wherever possible, she incorporates sustainable principles into her business. Within her collections, she uses organic cottons and low-impact dyes, and embraces new techniques and materials as they emerge. McCartney is conscious of making informed choices and acknowledges the importance of connecting with organizations that support the design industry in bringing about change.

In 2012, the company joined the Ethical Trading Initiative (ETI), which works to improve working conditions for people in fashion production around the world. The company has also partnered with the Natural Resource Defense Council (NRDC) in its 'Clean by Design' initiative. Clean by Design aims to reduce waste and emissions from production and manufacturing practices, predominately in less-developed countries. Stella McCartney is the first company to bring this initiative to Europe, working with her Italian mills to improve efficiency while decreasing water and energy use in textile production.

The company aims to reduce negative impacts across its entire operations, which includes reviewing and improving production practices and all other business operations. As the company states, 'We will continue to consider the impact we have on the planet as we design clothing, open stores and manufacture our products. We will probably never be perfect, but you can rest assured that we are always trying.'

<www.stellamccartney.com/experience/ stellas-world/sustainability/>

The life cycle of a garment

2.23

2.24

2.25

2.23 | Tote bag (made in Kenya), Spring 2011.

Stella McCartney created a range of handmade, recycled canvas tote bags in collaboration with the International Trade Centre's Ethical Fashion Initiative. The programme goes beyond charity and aims to generate economic independence for participating artisans. By providing work and training, sustainable livelihoods are being created within the most disadvantaged communities in Kenya.

2.24 | Bio soles, Fall 2010.

As part of her commitment to using innovative, ecological and luxurious leather alternatives, Stella McCartney launched a biodegradable rubber sole for the Fall 2010 collection and has continued to use this material in collections since.

2.25 | Organic cotton garments, Spring 2013.

Organic cotton is used as often as possible in Stella McCartney collections. Organic production uses water efficiently, does not involve harmful chemicals, restores and maintains soil health and promotes high social and working standards for farmers. In 2012, 34 per cent of all Stella McCartney denim and 36 per cent of all jersey was made from organic cotton, and 50 per cent of all the kidswear knit was organic.

Comparing two garments

For this exercise, you need to compare two different garments for their environmental and social performance. This is a good exercise to do in a team, especially if the members each come from different areas of fashion and textile production, for example, a knitter, a textile designer or a garment designer. An assessment can also be used as a tool for comparing an existing product against its redesigned version. In addition, it is a valuable exercise to do during the development of new design ideas.

2.26

First, choose two garments that you have previously designed and/or made for different occasions and have been developed from different fibre types.

Then, referring to the diagram of the 'Stages in the life cycle of a garment', shown on page 32, develop a life cycle map for each garment that includes all the major environmental and social impacts. Consider the inputs and outputs by referring to the diagram on page 37.

Next, referring to the diagram of a rating scale on page 39, plot the impacts for each of your garments according to where you think they should be rated. What do you see? Which garment has performed better overall? Where do you think each garment could improve?

2.26 | Bridal gown by Tammam.
Since 2007 the London-based ethical bridal and couture wear company Tammam have been using sustainable fabrics including organic and peace silks, and traditional craft skills to produce ready-to-wear and bespoke garments. The company has a fully monitored supply chain that embraces fair trade practices.

Finding information

Design

- Materials Assessment from The Apparel Coalition
<www.apparelcoalition.org/msi/>

- The Nike Environmental Design Tool
<www.nikebiz.com/responsibility/nikeenvironmentaldesigntool>

- Review of Life Cycle Assessments of Clothing and Textiles from Oakdene Hollins
<www.oakdenehollins.co.uk/textiles-clothing.php>

- Sustainable Clothing Action Plan from WRAP UK
<www.wrap.org.uk/content/sustainable-clothing-action-plan-1>

Production

- The Ethical Fashion Forum
<www.ethicalfashionforum.com/the-issues>

- Fair Wear Foundation
<www.fairwear.org/22/about/>

- Resources from the Clean Clothes Campaign
<www.cleanclothes.org/resources>

- Resources from the Ethical Trading Initiative
< www.ethicaltrade.org/resources>

- Textiles and Clothing: Environmental issues from Enterprise and Industry, European Commission
<http://ec.europa.eu/enterprise/sectors/textiles/environment/index_en.htm>

Distribution

- The Carbon Trust (UK)
<www.carbontrust.com>

- Act on CO_2 from The Carbon Calculator (UK)
<http://carboncalculator.direct.gov.uk/index.html>

- Greenhouse Gas Emissions from the United States Environmental Protection Agency
<www.epa.gov/climatechange/ghgemissions/>

Use

- Apparel Industry Life Cycle Carbon Mapping from the Business for Social Responsibility
< www.bsr.org/en/our-insights/report-view/apparel-industry-life-cycle-carbon-mapping>

- Sustainable Clothing Roadmap: Reducing the Environmental Impact of Clothes Cleaning from DEFRA (Department for Environment, Food and Rural Affairs) UK
<http://randd.defra.gov.uk/Default.aspx?Menu=Menu&Module=More&Location=None&Completed=0&ProjectID=16094>

End-of-life

- The Impact of the Second-hand Clothing Trade on Developing Countries from Oxfam UK
<http://policy-practice.oxfam.org.uk/publications/the-impact-of-the-second-hand-clothing-trade-on-developing-countries-112464>

- Textile Waste from the United States Environmental Protection Agency
<www.epa.gov/osw/conserve/materials/textiles.htm>

- WRAP (Waste and Resources Action Programme UK)
<www.wrap.org.uk/category/materials-and-products/textiles>

This chapter looks at the design phase as the starting point for addressing the negative environmental and ethical impacts associated with the phases of a garment's life cycle. Typically, a designer creates a garment in response to a design brief, which outlines specific criteria that have to be met to satisfy the expectations of consumers and the market. But to develop and produce the collection, the designer will need to identify and source a wide range of resources and services. This chapter will encourage you to reflect on the way you design garments, and to look at the techniques and processes that you may use in the manufacture of your products.

'I want people to appreciate that organic cotton can look and feel as good as conventional cotton, but the difference to cotton farmers and their families is huge.'
Katharine Hamnett

3

3.1 | 'Remnant' top by Lilia Yip, AW12/13.

Brighton-based Singaporean designer Lilia Yip used fabric remnants from her AW11/12 collection as fringing for a draped tencel top for her AW12/13 collection.

While you may feel confident that you can have an influence over reducing some of the impacts that occur during the design and production phases, it can be difficult to see how you can make an impact on what happens to a garment during the use and disposal phases. However, you can begin to address this if you have a better understanding of the people who buy and use your garments, and if you can bring this knowledge to your design process.

While you are gathering market and trends information, you can also be looking for information that reveals how wearers handle and manage clothing. This can be approached in a number of ways, but you can start by connecting with the people who buy the products that you design and make. As you elicit information from your wearers about their habits and rituals during the use and disposal phases, you will begin to draw together knowledge that can inform new design solutions. This can lead to an improved product performance for the wearer, the environment and society.

3.2

3.3

Closed-loop system of production

A closed-loop system of production provides an opportunity to reuse the materials of a product that has come to the end of its useful life. The materials are either considered compostable or are recycled into new products, typically of the same variety as the original product.

Design

3.4

Design-led approaches

As you begin to understand how wearers use and engage with the clothing that you develop, you can begin to consider design-led approaches that attempt to address specific problems. For example, a garment designed for longevity, as a slow approach to fashion, can embody specific functions that will encourage the wearer to use the garment in a particular way. You can employ a number of strategies to achieve this, for example, designing a garment that is multifunctional, or transformable, or highly durable, or may purposefully change with age, becoming different through use.

However, you can also choose to explore approaches that challenge the notion of slow fashion, and instead make use of technology and systems that speed up fashion. Here, you can use a closed-loop system of production and develop, for example, a garment that can be fully recycled or composted at the end of its useful life.

3.2 | Multifunctional top by Anna Ruohonen.

Paris-based Finnish designer Anna Ruohonen designs trans-seasonal garments that can be manufactured according to the wearer's needs, which avoids wasteful overproduction.

3.3 | Fake Natoo's Reclothing Bank–1 collection.

Na Zhang, founder of the Chinese fashion label Fake Natoo, reconstructs textile waste gathered from clothing banks to produce quirky and unique garments.

3.4 | 'A Cup of Tea Dress' by Lilia Yip.

Lilia Yip uses digital print techniques to design womenswear garments for the wearer to collect and keep as emotionally durable pieces.

How will your garment be used?

The success of a design-led approach relies upon your wearer engaging with the garment during the use phase, whether this involves participating with all of the features offered by a multifunctional garment or placing the garment in an appropriate recycling system. Regardless of which design-led approach you adopt, it is critical that the wearer complies with the strategy's aims and objectives for it to be considered successful. Understanding the relationship between the wearer and garment is therefore of critical importance to your design decisions.

3.5

3.5 and 3.6 | The 'Slot + Fold' collection by Cherelle Abrams.

For her Master of Design graduate collection, Abrams explored the concept of mix and match by developing a range of garments that can be split and reattached in different ways.

3.7 | The reversible 'Grow-Shrink-and-Turn-Coat' by Alice Payne.

This coat is constructed in modules that allow it to be adjusted depending on the wearer. Laser-cut holes allow for layers of cloth to be added or removed.

3.6

Look 1.   Look 2.   Look 3.   Look 4.   Look 5.   Look 6.

By encouraging an ongoing empathetic relationship between the wearer and the garment, the wearer is likely to care for, maintain and value the garment to the end of its useful life, thus reducing the impact of consumption. But while there are many ways to approach designing for empathy, it is fundamental that you understand the emotional cues that a garment can provide the wearer, and bring this insight to the design process. Designing for empathy requires you to listen to the people and communities that engage with your designs, and places an emphasis on a human-centred approach to designing.

An important starting point is to consider why people keep some items of clothing and not others. Although a number of researchers and designers are exploring this issue, it is evident that a single solution does not provide the answer, and that a number of techniques and responses are needed across the fashion industry. This is because the wearer's relationship with the clothing is an emotive one, so popular approaches adopted by designers have tended to stimulate an emotional response. For example, by revealing the provenance of a garment, either by sharing the profiles of the people involved in its creation or by providing the history of the previous owner of a vintage garment, the wearer is presented with a narrative that provides context and meaning, which engenders empathy.

For some wearers, the relationship with their clothing can be extended if a garment is perceived as individual or unique, perhaps because it has been personalized or is timeless or evolving. For example, a garment can be designed to be an adaptable product worn in different ways, through either simple or complex transformative processes, which will provide the wearer with two or three products in one. Alternatively, a connection can be established where there is a direct relationship between designer and wearer; a co-designed approach being adopted to translate the wearer's needs into a highly personalized and individual garment.

3.8

3.8 and 3.9 | Pachacuti's traceable supply chain.

As part of the Geo Fair Trade project, Pachacuti is working to build trust between producer and consumer by providing a traceable sustainable provenance of its whole supply chain using Quick Response (QR) code technology. This allows consumers to trace the support they give to groups of producers and to individual weavers.

3.9

3.10 | Beate Godager's White collection, AW12.

Danish-based designer Beate Godager approaches fashion design from a conceptual position drawing on art, deconstruction and tailoring. Her designs are minimal and timeless.

3.10

```
NAME:ZIP SWEATER          NAME:WOOL STRETCH PANTS
ART.NO:BG005              ART.NO:BG008
```

Designing for empathy

Your task is to observe different wearers interacting with clothing. You can also act out and experience a garment from the perspective of your wearer. Capture the information using a variety of tools, for example, a camera, a video, questionnaires, focus groups or the use of diaries. See the 'Human-Centered Toolkit' from IDEO for methods and approaches to human-centred design. (See <www.hcdconnect.org>.)

Analyse and reflect on the information you have gathered. What have you learned? Brainstorm your solutions – how can you bring your research into your garment ideas?

Then develop toiles and samples using your research. Conduct tests and reflect on the outcomes. Do your garments encourage empathy? Can they sustain the wearer's engagement?

3.11 | The Purse project by Tara Baoth Mooney.

Tara Baoth Mooney draws on the emotional attachment that people can have with textile objects that carry personal memories. The purse was a treasured gift from mother to daughter, which Baoth Mooney reinterpreted into a wearable, functional and meaningful piece.

3.12 and 3.13 | User-centred testing by Eunjeong Jeon.

These pieces, from designer and researcher Eunjeong Jeon, provide the wearer with comfort and changeability and were designed using a process of user-centred testing.

3.11

3.12

3.13

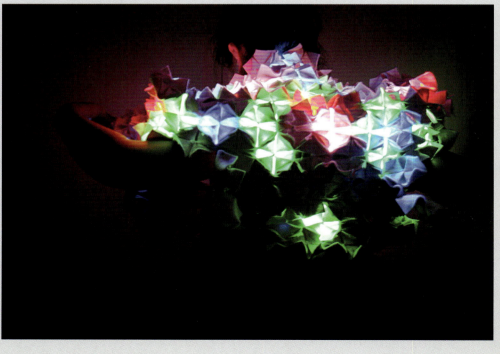

For many fashion designers, the creation of a collection begins with the fabric and textile techniques. A fabric is typically selected for its weight, texture, drape and handle, as well as its aesthetic appeal and price. But it is becoming increasingly important to consider the environmental and social impacts connected to materials and textiles techniques.

As we have already described, a huge range of environmental and ethical impacts are created from the production of raw fibre to fabric, and on to the use and disposal phases once the fabric has been manufactured into a garment. The picture is complicated further by the impacts that are associated with manipulating and enhancing fabrics, for example, finishing and surface treatments, and embellishment techniques.

3.14

3.14 | AW12 Artisanal collection from Maison Martin Margiela.

A range is often constructed using reclaimed clothing and found and discarded objects. This range from Maison Martin Margiela incorporated vintage baseball gloves alongside lace.

Design

Fibres and fabrics

3.15

The majority of materials, regardless of fibre type, incur impacts at some point in a garment's life cycle, whether in terms of the large volumes of petrochemicals used to manufacture them (as with polyester) or the large amounts of energy and water used in washing a garment (as in cotton). A number of studies and life cycle assessments have been conducted on fibre types such as cotton and polyester, and a number of guides and resources outline the impacts of each fibre. It is useful to understand these as you begin sourcing and selecting your fabrics. For example, fabrics can be derived from organic or renewable sources and may be grown or processed using fair trade practices, while new textile developments have led to the creation of manufactured materials that may be considered low impact, recyclable or biodegradable.

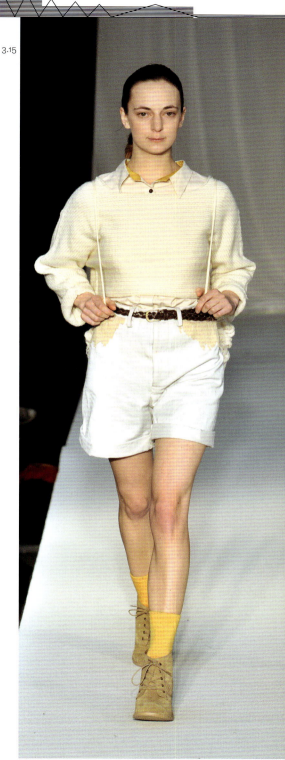

3.15 | Natural dye shorts and organic cotton shirt by Amy Ward, 2012.

Recent graduate Amy Ward uses organic fibres and natural techniques in her collection. Ward sourced vegetable dyes extracted from food waste, and used organic, fair trade and eco-friendly fabrics and yarns.

Textile processes

Fibres and fabrics can be manipulated to achieve different effects using techniques such as knitting, embroidery, digital and screen-printing methods, and finishing processes including laminating and coating. Each of these will contribute to the impact of a garment at some point in its life cycle, and you need to be aware of these issues in your preparation work. For example, a number of textile treatments, such as bleaching and dyeing, have traditionally involved the use of chemicals, but new developments now enable some processes to be conducted with a reduced or minimal impact – fabrics can be dyed using low-impact dyes and processes, or natural dyes, or may remain neutral in shade, playing instead on the natural characteristics of the fibre.

3.16

3.17

3.16 | 'Travelling Circus Jacket' by Jan Knibbs.

Embroiderer Jan Knibbs incorporates fabric remnants into her work and embellishes existing garments using appliqué techniques.

3.17 and 3.18 | Hand-stitched garments from Alabama Chanin.

Focusing on the principles of sustainability and a slow fashion movement, designer Natalie Chanin established her fashion label Alabama Chanin in the Florence region of Alabama in the USA. Local artisans produce handmade products using reclaimed and organic materials, and traditional craft techniques.

Design

3.18

3.19

3.20

Sourcing and selecting

During the design phase, as you select the fabrics, trimmings, processes and services that will be used during manufacturing, you will have to base your decisions on 'trade-offs', which means basing your design choices on what you know will produce the least impact. However, it is only by understanding the bigger picture – that is, the whole life cycle of your designed garment – that you can attempt to reduce its negative impacts. There are, however, tools and resources that can help you. Sourcing departments can benefit from research presented in specialist industry magazines such as the *Ecotextile News* (UK), which covers advances in new fibre development, cleaner and more efficient dye and print technology, transparent tracking and labelling systems, and so on. A number of specialist fabric and yarn suppliers, ethical manufacturers and industry organizations can also help with sourcing.

Organic cotton

Organic clothing and textiles are made using environmentally friendly processes that are applied from field to manufacture. In the fashion industry, the Global Organic Textile Standard (GOTS) or Soil Association (UK) will work with designers and companies to help support and monitor sustainable practices and standards.

3.21

Fair trade fabrics

Fair trade aims to support the livelihoods of people, often based in rural or developing communities, by paying fair prices for their goods and services while reinvesting profit back into the local community. When consumers see the FAIRTRADE Mark on cotton, it means that farmers in developing countries have received a fair price for their cotton. It is, however, important to remember that FAIRTRADE certification does not yet cover the whole manufacturing process of a garment.

3.19 | Julika Works SS11 collection.
Based in Iceland, the knitwear brand Julika Works uses certified and fair trade materials for luxury knit pieces.

3.20 | The C.L.A.S.S showroom in Milan.
The C.L.A.S.S (Creativity, Lifestyle and Sustainable Synergy) showrooms in Milan, London, Helsinki and Madrid each host an eco-library. You can see the latest eco-friendly fabrics and yarns, and get advice on how and where to source materials and services.

3.21 | The FAIRTRADE Certified Cotton mark.
The FAIRTRADE Mark is a registered independent certification label. The Mark on cotton means that cotton farmers in developing communities have received a fair and stable price and an additional fair trade premium, which they choose how to invest in their businesses and communities for a sustainable future.

Using mono-materials

A variety of approaches can be used to divert discarded garments and textile waste away from landfill at the point of disposal. One option is to mechanically recycle a garment's materials to use in the production of a new by-product material. Recovered pre- and post-consumer textile waste is shredded and spun to form the new material, which is used in a range of industrial and domestic products including wipers, padding and stuffing. But although this is a beneficial method for using waste material, there are some issues that make this process difficult. For example, some textile waste is considered unacceptable because the garment is contaminated with unsuitable fibres, surface treatments or fittings. Moreover, the true value of the material being recycled during this process is reduced or 'downcycled'.

By using an uncontaminated mono-material – a fabric of a single fibre type – in a garment's production, there is a greater opportunity to successfully engage in recycling. While working with a mono-material, you can also experiment with embellishment techniques, such as laser-cutting or needle-punching, which can provide detail without contaminating the fibre. Working in this way can then lead you to identify and test a variety of techniques and processes that can aesthetically alter the appearance of a mono-material without changing its composition.

Moreover, if a garment is designed so that its component parts can be easily separated, especially if some parts are constructed from other materials, this further increases the opportunity to recycle it. The separated materials can either be recycled in the manufacture of new products, forming a closed-loop system of production, or can be composted if they are suitable.

3.22

3.23

3.24

3.22 | Hand-knitted garments by Ainokainen.

The sheep wool used in knitwear from Finnish label Ainokainen is sourced locally and coloured using natural plant and vegetable dyes.

3.23 and 3.24 | Removable prints collection by Reinfinity, Anne Noodegraaf and More Tea Vicar.

Netherlands-based researcher Fioen van Balgooi has developed a removable print process for textile prints. When the fabric has had the ink removed from it, it can be either recycled or reprinted.

Using mono-materials

Fibres that have typically achieved success in closed-loop systems of production are those developed synthetically. The reason for this success may lie in the relatively similar qualities of the original fibre and its secondary product when remanufactured in larger quantities, which cannot currently be achieved with all fibre types. For example, while wool can be recycled, it may often need blending with a virgin fibre to retain its quality. However, as recycling technology and the relationship between manufacturers and textile recyclers improve, richer and more diverse opportunities begin to emerge.

3.25

3.26

3.27

3.30

3.30 | 'Stylized 027' paper garment by Tao Kurihara, 2007.

As a replacement for fabric, paper can be used to create one-off, disposable fashion pieces that can be recycled. This paper garment, by Tao Kurihara for Comme des Garçons, is part of the collection of the Kyoto Costume Museum.

3.28

3.29

3.25–3.29 | 'Mono Finishing' project by Dr Kate Goldsworthy, 2008–2010.

Dr Kate Goldsworthy has been exploring finishing processes to improve the aesthetic appearance of polyester-based fabrics. The aim is to preserve the fabric as a mono-material so that it can remain uncontaminated for recycling.

Annika Matilda Wendelboe

3.31

3.32

3.33

Swedish fashion designer Annika Matilda Wendelboe began her own fashion label in 2007, producing sustainable fashion that is both versatile and timeless. She is one of the first designers to produce a collection that uses Cradle to Cradle CertifiedCM materials, which allow the garments to be safely composted or placed in a closed-loop system at the point of disposal.

3.31 | Annika Matilda Wendelboe.

3.32–3.34 | Multifunctional garments by Annika Matilda Wendelboe.

Many of Wendelboe's creations can be worn in a number of ways. Wendelboe uses creative construction and draping techniques so that, for example, a collar can be used as a scarf or a hood.

What first inspired you to bring sustainability into your fashion collections?

I have always loved creating fashion, but contributing to the mountain of waste, supporting the exploitation of the earth and humans, made me ashamed of my job. It is a much nicer feeling to know that what I produce is leaving positive footprints.

How has your design and production process changed in order to meet your environmental and ethical goals?

Eagerly awaiting the perfect world with only truly good materials, I meanwhile aim to make long-lasting products. High-quality fabrics of course, but also versatile designs so you can, for example, transform a jacket into a dress into a skirt and so on. That way it takes longer before you grow tired of it!

Design

3·34

Annika Matilda Wendelboe

Have there been any challenges in bringing sustainability into your collections? Has it been difficult sourcing materials and resources?

The choice of fabrics that are healthy is still a bit limited (for a small producer like me), and that means a good challenge in the design process. The collection with Cradle to Cradle fabrics is entirely made of upholstery fabrics, and there were no C2C-certified zippers and hardly any buttons so I had to find other solutions for that.

What would you next like to explore or bring into the collections?

I am very curious to find a way to rent fashion and have some sort of deposition system for the materials, to make people return their clothes when they are done with them. I am doing research on it to see how it can best be done.

Do you have any tips or advice for a fashion student who may want to produce a sustainable fashion collection?

Networking, cooperating and sharing knowledge with others has helped me a lot. There are initiatives to co-buy with other designers if minimum quantities are high. And for me, it is a great source of joy and energy to feel that I am trying to make good – not just less bad!

3.35

<www.matildawendelboe.se>

Cradle to Cradle CertifiedCM is a certification mark of MBDC, LLC.
< www.c2ccertified.org/>

3.35 and 3.36 | C2C Certified garments by Annika Matilda Wendelboe.
Wendelboe uses organic and C2C CertifiedCM materials in her collections and all of the garments are sewn in Sweden. Consumers can also find clothing care instructions on her website.

3.36

The methods used to produce a garment can vary greatly depending upon the size of the company and the market for which the garments are being produced. But whether it is a small-scale local designer label or a large international brand that produces garments offshore, what stays more or less consistent is the process of production. This chapter looks specifically at two areas in the production process: pattern-making and toiling, and garment construction. Although these activities have a wide range of impacts, this chapter introduces a number of improvements that can be made.

'Conservation of fabric, labour and time are part of my design decisions. It is important that my work does not perpetuate waste; that economy is factored into design. The width of the fabric and the design layout help to minimize waste.'

Yeohlee Teng, founder of Yoehlee

4.1 | Vivienne Westwood works with producers in Kenya on her Ethical Fashion Africa collection.

The bags in Vivienne Westwood's Ethical Fashion Africa collection are handcrafted using recycled materials by marginalized communities of women in Nairobi, Kenya. In collaboration with the International Trade Centre (ITC) and their Ethical Fashion Initiative, Vivienne Westwood is able to support disadvantaged women who continue to supply high-quality products for the company.

4

4.2

It is through the pattern-making and toiling phase of the production process that a design idea is truly brought to life. During this phase, the final look of the garment, its appropriate construction methods and its material and labour requirements are all determined. But it can also be the point at which many negative impacts are created.

The design and production process for a garment involves a generic sequence of activities. A garment is sketched, a paper pattern is drafted, a toile is produced, a marker is made, the full sample range is cut and made, and then selected garments are manufactured for retail. During all these phases, it is important for you to look for opportunities for materials and resources to be used wisely and efficiently. To do this, you will need to identify all types of waste that are created during the production phase, and look further down the pipeline to see what other impacts may arise because of the decisions made at this point.

4.2 and 4.3 | North Face Zero Waste project, 2010.

Menswear designer David Telfer explores a variety of approaches to efficiency through creative pattern-making solutions. In 2010, David collaborated with The North Face and TED (Textile Environment Design) on a zero-wase project.

4.3

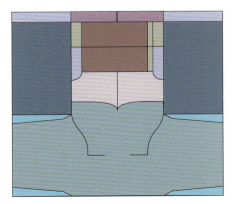

Reducing textile waste

One of the biggest issues associated with the production phase is the creation of unnecessary textile waste. In the 'cut, make and trim' (CMT) process, up to 15 per cent of the fabric is wasted through uncreative approaches to pattern-making. Conventional pattern-making methods produce paper pattern pieces that are often difficult to lay efficiently within the full width and length of the fabric, which then leads to the creation of textile waste during manufacture. Even with the use of computer aided design (CAD) pattern-cutting software programs, which produce a marker using the pattern pieces in an efficient and cost-effective way, waste is unavoidable.

You can, however, begin to address textile waste in your practice by looking for the negative 'outputs' that emerge when you are in the fashion workshop. For example, rather than (re)producing several toiles to test one design idea, you can rework the same toile multiple times. This may seem a small change to make within your practice, but a wealth of small changes can bring about a significant reduction in textile waste. It is also possible to minimize or avoid textile waste by exploring zero-waste approaches to pattern-cutting (see pages 80 and 83).

4.4

4.4 | SS12 'Flyaway top' and 'Two-tone pant' from Titania Inglis.

Winner of the 2012 Ecco Domani Fashion Foundation Award for Sustainable Design, New York-based designer, Titania Inglis uses a creative approach to pattern-making to develop fashion garments that are graphic, minimal and wearable.

Cut, make and trim (CMT)

A garment manufacturing process that is provided by an external company using supplied materials.

Creative approaches to pattern-cutting

It is also possible to delay a garment's journey to landfill by improving its quality through a considered and creative approach to pattern-making. For example, a multifunctional garment could allow the wearer to create several 'looks' using a single garment. But if a garment is multifunctional, there is a need for the garment to fit and transform well when changing from one form to another. For this to succeed, the designer/pattern-maker needs to understand the functionality of use, which requires a reflective approach to design and production involving experimentation and engaging in methods such as user testing.

Alternatively, a garment can be developed to fit more than one body size at a time, becoming multisized. This requires an understanding of the body and how the garment moves and adapts to accommodate differential sizing, which should be considered and addressed while developing the paper pattern.

It is important to appreciate that the design, pattern-making and toiling phases should be considered as an interconnected process. Rather than seeing the design phase as a precursor to the pattern-making/toiling phase (a linear process), moving backwards and forwards between design, pattern-making and toiling will provide an opportunity to address some of the issues discussed here. Moreover, if you consider that the design of a garment is not a fixed outcome of the design phase, but the start of a conversation that continues into pattern-making and toiling, truly novel solutions can arise.

4.5

4.5 | Elementum Summer Collection by Daniela Pais.

Daniela Pais established the label Elementum after graduating with a Masters from the Design Academy Eindhoven. This collection is made up of nine component pieces that can be worn in many different configurations.

4.6

4.6 | Wool jacket and digital print by Janice Egerton and Dino Soteriou.

Using simple geometric shapes, designers Janice Egerton and Dino Soteriou have created multifunctional garments with digital print techniques.

4.7

4.8

4.7 and 4.8 | Zero-waste dress by Mark Liu.

Australian designer and researcher Mark Liu uses laser-cut decorative edge finishes that interlock before the garment pieces are cut out of the fabric.

Zero-waste techniques

Avoiding fabric waste through efficiency in pattern-making played an important part in the production of early historical garments. The ancient Greek chiton and the Japanese kimono both involved simple panel lines that enabled the garment to be cut from the cloth with little waste. This was originally done for economic reasons since cloth was expensive. However, as fashion began to fit more closely to the body, shaped pattern pieces were required. With a combination of straight and curved lines, pattern pieces now no longer lock together efficiently. This results in the creation of positive and negative space in the cloth, and it is the negative pieces, or scraps, that become the discarded waste.

As a starting point, it is useful to reflect on earlier examples of historical garments so you can apply tried and tested methods for minimizing fabric waste. This will then lead you to experiment with more complex garment silhouettes and styles, some of which will involve shaping.

Although textile waste is created at various stages of a garment's life cycle, it is possible to minimize and 'design out' fabric waste during the pattern-making and toiling phase by engaging in zero-waste techniques. To do this, the designer/pattern-maker needs to be able to move confidently between the three-dimensional form and two-dimensional pattern-making, going back and forth until, through design choices, fabric waste is minimized.

While concepts like these could be explored further within the industry, traditional approaches to pattern-making, such as draping, which is typically applied in couture, often begin with the application of one piece of cloth that is moulded directly on to the mannequin. The fabric is sculpted into a form using a series of cuts, folds and pleats, often without cutting much or any fabric away. This approach is evident in the work of couturier Madeleine Vionnet.

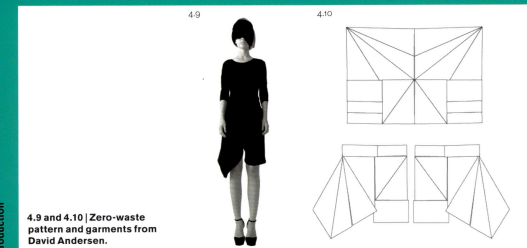

4.9

4.10

4.9 and 4.10 | Zero-waste pattern and garments from David Andersen.

4.11

4.12

4.11 | Zero-waste garments by Fiona Mills.

Nottingham Trent University MA graduate Fiona Mills uses a zero-waste approach to design and pattern-making by experimenting with geometric shapes and one-piece lengths.

4.12 | A Japanese kimono from the mid-nineteenth century.

The rectangular pattern pieces used in the production of a kimono created during the second half of the nineteenth century.

Zero-waste techniques

Apart from the opportunity to eliminate or reduce waste during pattern-making, technology has enabled fashion producers to explore a zero-waste approach at the point of construction. This approach usually requires manufacturing the garment pieces directly without the need for cutting from a piece of cloth. A number of designers are beginning to explore techniques that involve directly weaving the pieces of a garment into the correct size and shape, providing the possibility to dramatically reduce the textile waste that occurs during production.

4.13

4.13 | Zero-waste project by Line Sander Johansen, 2008.

A graduate of the Kolding School of Design, designer Line Sander Johansen uses a production technique that creates little or no waste since the garment pieces are woven to shape directly on the loom.

Production

4.14

4.15

4.14 and 4.15 | Purple zero-waste dress by Line Sander Johansen, 2008.

Made from 100 per cent woven elastic thread, Line Sander Johansen's zero-waste dress is seen here in its two-dimensional development phase and as a three-dimensional piece on the body.

Working with geometric shapes

By using a geometric shape, such as a square, rectangle or triangle, it is possible to use cloth efficiently with little or no waste. The aim of this exercise is for you to develop new design ideas that use fabric efficiently by experimenting with a geometric shape. At the end, you will have the start of a sketchbook of ideas.

Begin by choosing a geometric shape. Draw and cut out a template of your shape in two different sizes, so that you have both a small and a large shape.

Using a piece of remnant cloth, draw around the templates and cut out a few of each shape, making sure that you cut more smaller shapes than larger ones. Be careful not to waste the fabric and only cut what you think you will need and use.

Manipulate your cut fabric shapes on the mannequin to see if you can create a top and a skirt. Use folds and pleats to make interesting sculptural forms, as in origami. To begin with, focus on creating a section of a garment, for example, a sleeve or a front panel.

Using pins, try the following ideas: build up layers of larger and smaller shapes, making incisions in the layers to reveal the underlying pieces; make a cut in a shape and twist it, repeating this several times and then pinning the shapes together; and cut a slit in one shape and slot in the smaller shapes.

Unpin and re-pin your work, photographing and sketching the experiments as you go. Try the exercise with different weights, textures and colours of cloth.

4.16

4.16−4.21 | The 132 5. ISSEY MIYAKE collection , 2010.

This collection emerged from a collaboration between the designer, textile designer and pattern engineers at Issey Miyake's Reality Lab and a computer scientist at the University of Tsukuba. Using a geometric shape cut from a single piece of recycled polyester fabric, each garment can be worn in a number of different ways. The images show how the garments look both in two-dimensional and three-dimensional forms.

4.17

4.18

4.19

4.20

4.21

This section specifically focuses on how the life cycle of a garment can be extended and improved if attention is given to the approaches and techniques used for its construction. Discussing concepts that range from techniques for slow approaches to fashion, to advances in new technology that help to reduce overproduction, this section introduces strategies that aim to tackle some of the issues arising from the manufacturing process. The discussion is connected to and expanded further in the next chapter on distribution, particularly in relation to ethical and fair trade practices in production.

4.22

4.23

4.22 | A jacket from the 'Hand-Me-Down' collection from Howies.

Using high-quality materials, 'Hand-Me-Down' garments from Howies are designed to last for ten years, which has required a considered design process that involves looking for and correcting potential weak points.

4.23 | The Unisex #2 collection from RAD by Rad Hourani.

Paris-based designer Rad Hourani produces trans-seasonal garments that can be worn by both men and women.

4.24

Construction methods

Once the final sample garment has been developed and approved for manufacture, the design is ready to go into production. A number of techniques and processes will be involved in manufacturing, but when considering the environmental and ethical impacts of your designs, it is beneficial to reflect on the construction methods used to make a garment. For example, a knitted garment can be manufactured either by sewing together garment pieces that have been cut from machine-knitted fabric, by knitting the shaped garment pieces and then stitching these together, or by knitting the whole garment with minimal seaming.

Inexpensive garments are often noted for being poorly constructed, which typically leads to clothing that becomes misshapen, badly fitting or unserviceable. This can be due to the quality of the fabric, but the seams used to make low-cost clothing tend to be insufficient and fragile, often breaking down during washing or general wear and tear.

By using quality materials and appropriate processes, you can give garments the chance of an extended life cycle, which can be beneficial to your consumer. Unique construction methods applied in the made-to-measure sectors can also enable the wearer to adapt, alter or repair a custom-made garment.

4.24 | 'Ginza' modular dress from Allenomis.

Annalisa Simonella moved from architecture to fashion to develop the Allenomis label. Simonella's garments are designed with more than one function in mind – each can be worn in multiple ways and/or incorporate responsive materials and technologies.

4.25

Developments in construction techniques

Advances in technology have enabled producers – particularly of sports, street and outdoor wear – to develop large volumes of clothing that is highly functional, adaptable or customizable. Moreover, the notion of providing a customizable service is transforming the way garments are constructed across many sectors of the industry. The fashion industry is now beginning to supply wearers with products that suit individual needs. Wearers can order and customize products online directly from the supplier, make designer clothing at home using kits, or engage in DIY approaches supported by online forums and blog sites. The methods used to make fashion garments are being challenged, and techniques that can support personalization, including digital manufacturing processes such as rapid prototyping, are opening up a wealth of creative opportunities for both designer and wearer. These approaches will be explored further in the next chapter.

Rapid prototyping

Rapid prototyping is a process of making a model or component that uses computer aided design (CAD) technology, including three-dimensional printing – the model is built, or 'printed', layer upon layer.

4.25 and 4.26 | The Crystal Collection by Naomi Bailey-Cooper.

Slow fashion concepts can involve preparing garments for ageing. The Crystal Collection from graduate Naomi Bailey-Cooper changes and evolves over time as the decorative crystal formations grow within the garment. See Chapter 6 for further discussions on designing garments for ageing.

4.26

In a challenge to models of mass-production and consumption, there has been a move towards the use of 'slow design' strategies. The notion of slow fashion supports meeting the real needs of the individual, the community and the environment in a way that, among other things, counteracts the quick response time typically used in mass-manufacturing. Designing durable products is one way of helping drive the movement for slower patterns of consumption.

'Design for durability' in fashion begins by understanding what is needed for a garment to be durable. The notion of durability can mean different things to different people; one wearer may believe that durability exists in a made-to-measure suit, while another wearer may believe that durability can be found in a pair of denim jeans. Individual value systems vary greatly, so it is important to understand consumers' expectations of durability in relation to the garments you design. Although durability in fashion can be achieved in many ways, it is a combination of approaches that helps a garment last – for example, garments can have a timeless aesthetic and also be effectively cared for and maintained during use. However, using appropriate and considered materials and construction techniques in the manufacture of the garment makes an important contribution to enhancing durability through use.

In haute couture, the processes and details applied in the garment construction phase are often distinguishable from those of their ready-to-wear counterparts. Couture garments include a variety of features that are 'built-in' to help extend the life cycle of a garment. Dress shields are used as a method of protecting the fabric in areas of high wear and tear, such as the underarm area of a sleeve. In addition, where different sections of a garment meet at a junction, the fabric edges are usually sewn down by hand with microscopic stitches, further strengthening the seams.

Examples of haute couture garments from the 1950s reveal that the preparation for (later) alteration work was often included in a garment as it was being created. However, when alterations were made to garments, fabrics were not usually cut or removed. This meant that the garment could be reconfigured in a number of ways over a period of many years, for example, if there was a need for updating or upsizing.

4.27

4.28

4.27 | The 'Kurkistus' dress from Marimekko's Classics collection.

Made from Öko-Tex 100 per cent cotton, the classically shaped Kurkistus dress from Marimekko incorporates the vintage 'Nadja' print, designed by Vuokko Eskolin-Nurmesniemi, which the company has been using in Iloinen takki dresses and coin purses since the 1950s.

4.28 | Livia Firth wearing Valentino for the 2012 Green Carpet Challenge.

For the 2012 Green Carpet Challenge, Livia Firth wore a dress made from a blend of silk and recycled PET plastic by couture designer Valentino.

4.29

4.30

4.29 | Susan Dimasi.

4.30 | MATERIALBYPRODUCT SS08.

The MATERIALBYPRODUCT signature 'mark-making' is demonstrated in the runway look from the SS08 collection.

4.31 and 4.32 | MATERIALBYPRODUCT design process shots.

Materialbyproduct work with both the positive and negative spaces within cloth to create high-quality garments, which embrace elements of tailoring, mark-making and craftsmanship.

Designer Susan Dimasi established the Australian-based fashion label MATERIALBYPRODUCT in Melbourne in 2004. Famous for its signature systematic techniques for marking, cutting and joining cloth, the label produces luxury garments that are sold nationally and internationally.

What first inspired you to create sustainable fashion?

I wanted to establish new approaches to (1) artisan craft and (2) manufacturing for the twenty-first century. Sustainability is a significant twenty-first-century concern. However, sustainability is not the feature of my practice, it is an aspect of it.

Why have you produced fashion garments that use a zero-waste approach?

My approach to sustainability is a very sincere and personal one. It comes from two things. The first thing is a love for an uncut piece of cloth, which I think is the ultimate garment and modular design object. Examples include draperies from antiquity, saris and, my favourite wardrobe item, a scarf. An uncut piece of cloth can also be a blanket, a curtain, a partition.

This love of an uncut piece of cloth collides with my second love: tailoring. I feel that as soon as I cut a piece of cloth, I have essentially ruined it! I then follow the materialbyproduct (MBP) cut, with the MBP join. The join brings the cut piece of cloth back together in a very particular way, almost back to an uncut piece of cloth. The MBP join is invested with enormous respect.

4.31

4.32

What is your design process?

To conceptualize a system and develop it by hand, resulting in an artisan by-product or 'fashion line'. Now, I am in the process of digitizing and mechanizing artisan systems to establish new approaches to manufacturing for the twenty-first century. These resulting by-products will form two new lines – 'Limited Edition' and 'Production'.

What opportunities or difficulties have you encountered by bringing sustainability into your collections?

One of the systems of cutting that I have innovated produces little or zero waste. However, when I am asked to speak in the sustainability context, I always stress that not everything I make is zero waste, and not everything I do 'ticks the box'.

Change. Every time I change or experiment, the outcome is not necessarily zero waste. Yes, I have a system for transforming all waste into new garments, but the commercialization of all these new garment types is another challenge again.

What would you like to explore or bring into the collections next?

I'm developing a new system called 'Accumulation'. The Accumulation system is one system whereby garments can have additional detail or embellishment built up over time. In the current 'Bleed' project, a slip dress has been hand drawn on with Texta marker pen. Detail accumulates in two ways: (1) each season more drawing is added to the slip dress, and (2) wear also contributes to the Accumulation process. Contact with the skin and body makes a Texta drawing bleed. So the wearer is also part of the process of building up additional detail. I am currently developing my second project using the Accumulation system, called 'Embodiment'.

As part of a globalized industry, fashion producers make use of distribution networks that enable them to buy and use resources and services from anywhere in the world. However, this system creates a variety of environmental and ethical impacts that may at times be invisible to the designer and producer. Discussed from two perspectives – production and retail – the chapter introduces a range of approaches that aim either to reduce the need for transportation or to minimize the impacts that arise from transporting goods.

'The greatest challenge is that we work in isolated places, in villages using craft skills and basic technology. We produce slowly; that creates the maximum number of jobs and incomes.'

Safia Minney, founder of People Tree

5.1 | A piece from Iris van Herpen's Crystallization collection, SS10.

Iris van Herpen uses rapid prototyping technology to print garments into a three-dimensional form. The elaborate and intricate pieces create no waste since each item is printed individually using a process that repeatedly adds material in layers until the form is created.

This section looks specifically at the impacts related to the shipping of materials and resources between suppliers, makers and producers. Although there are environmental impacts associated with the shipping of goods across and between continents, countries and states, there are also numerous impacts that affect the livelihood and well-being of many people and communities.

Reducing environmental impacts

Efficiency in fashion production usually involves sourcing materials and services that are available for the best possible price, which often requires working with offshore suppliers and manufacturers. Although this seems to make economic sense, environmental impacts arise from the transportation of goods whether they are moved by plane, ship, train or truck. Transport systems draw on natural resources for fuel, leading to an increase in air pollution and the release of greenhouse gases.

As a designer, the first step towards improvement is to gather research from your suppliers and find out what methods of transportation they are using. You may find that some components are shipped from overseas locations because they are cheaper than locally available products. Such decisions are based purely on economics, often involving only a minimal saving, and do not take into account the larger environmental costs that arise from some transportation methods. Making use of greener distribution methods, for example delivery lorries that run on biofuels, is a step in the right direction, but it is important to understand the broader impacts of the transportation methods you use.

5.2

5.2 and 5.3 | Looks from Suno's 2012 (left) and 2013 (opposite) Resort collections.

The New York-based label Suno produces its garments in Kenya using kangas, traditional African sarong-like pieces of cotton fabric decorated with traditional prints and patterns.

5.3

Reducing your carbon footprint

The term 'carbon footprint' refers to the measurement of carbon dioxide (CO_2) and other gases that are released into the atmosphere as a consequence of the things we do. CO_2 emissions are released from fossil fuels, such as oil and gas, which are used to create energy that powers sewing machines, washing machines and transportation. Moreover, greenhouse gases are emitted during the production of some raw fibres. You can calculate your own carbon footprint – this can lead you to look for different approaches that will either offset this figure or reduce it. For more information, go to:

- The Carbon Trust (UK)

- The Carbon Calculator (UK)
  <http://carboncalculator.direct.gov.uk/index.html>

- The United States Environmental Protection Agency
  <www.epa.gov/climatechangeghgemissions/>

Understanding ethical impacts

In addition to environmental impacts, human and social concerns also arise from transporting materials for fashion production, particularly when working with offshore suppliers and producers. Historically, offshore relationships were fraught with difficulty as producers struggled to manage the conditions under which people worked to manufacture their products. Over the last two decades, however, a growing number of groups have emerged to offer support and advice to producers. These organizations can provide information on selecting appropriate manufacturers and suppliers so you can be sure that the people in your supply chain have fair wages and working conditions.

Problems can occur onshore as well as offshore. In Australia, the Ethical Clothing Australia organization provides fashion labels with assistance to conduct monitoring that ensures mandatory New South Wales and Victoria State government requirements for the fair and safe employment of outworkers and factory workers are met. The organization even goes one step further, offering to guide a fashion label through its voluntary accreditation and labelling system, which is designed to encourage and promote ethical production within Australia.

5.4

5.4 | SOKO production facility.

SOKO Kenya is an ethical clothing production facility based in Ukunda, which manufactures fashion garments for international labels and brands. The company works with local cooperatives and craftspeople, and supports the local community by providing fair employment and training.

Corporate social responsibility (CSR)

A CSR policy is developed by a company as a method for setting out the standards, aims and goals to which a company adheres. Many producers and businesses generate an annual CSR report as a mechanism for informing their key stakeholders, including the public, about the achievements and progress that have been made within the company. As a self-regulating policy, this typically relies on a company setting out standards in relation to ethical and/or sustainable business practices, which can vary in significance from one company to the next.

Creating a transparent supply chain

While there are organizations and associations to help you establish good partners and networks, it can be difficult to create a transparent supply chain. Although it is possible and manageable to gather this information at a local, small-scale level, it can be a complex undertaking within large-scale fashion manufacturing. There are now, however, a number of companies and schemes that use new technologies to help you track and trace the movement of goods. The company Historic Futures developed a new online platform called 'string' so that producers and retailers could manage the traceability of their supply chain. This platform allows users to gather information about the products and services that they buy from suppliers and producers, and then use this to build a traceable production history for a garment from the production of raw fibre right through to the finished product. This information can then be shared with the consumer through an Internet link.

Informing the public and other stakeholders about your intentions and improvements is important and can be declared through corporate social responsibility (CSR) reporting. Some large brands, such as Nike, have been able to use corporate reporting processes as a method for motivating changes within the supply chain of their subcontractors.

Defining ethical fashion and fair trade fashion

As we have already described, the term 'ethical fashion' refers to clothing whose production meets set standards in relation to human and labour rights, for example, those of the International Labour Organization. Ethical trade is about having confidence that the products we buy have not been made at the expense of workers in global supply chains. It involves companies taking a series of recognized steps to identify problems and improve working conditions throughout their supply chains.

The term 'fair trade' fashion relates to the making of fashion and related items as a method for creating social development. It aims to support the livelihoods of people who often live in rural or developing communities, paying fair prices for goods and services, and reinvesting the profit into the local community. Consumers can recognize this when they see the FAIRTRADE certification mark label.

Non-governmental and industry organizations and associations that offer advice and support include the Ethical Trading Initiative, Fair Wear Foundation, Fair Labor Association, Clean Clothes Campaign, World Fair Trade Organization and Fairtrade International.

5.5

Large- versus small-scale production

The debate surrounding the advantages and disadvantages of large- versus small-scale production is a topical question for the fashion industry. The homogenized fashion often seen in the high street is usually a consequence of large-scale manufacturing, and a number of studies have clearly shown that one possible future direction for the fashion industry could be a growth in smaller fashion enterprises run at a local level. At the local level, it also becomes possible to cultivate the production of garments alongside those of services; a localized fashion industry can begin to grow into a sustainable community of skilled artisans, producers, suppliers and service providers who can think at a global level, yet act a local level.

In the drive to lead consumers to buy less, the perfect opportunity arises for an increase in new, inventive design services that focus on, for instance, repairing, remodelling and leasing garments, which shifts the fashion industry towards product service systems (PSSs). The value-added benefits of such a system provide consumers with a rich mix of personalized and professional services that is responsive to their needs.

5.5 | Everlasting Sprout AW12/13.

Alongside its production of ready-to-wear collections, the Japanese fashion label Everlasting Sprout offers kits with instructions and materials so that consumers can make their own garments.

5.6 | 'Stripy T' and 'Wrap Trouser' from Antiform AW11.

The UK fashion label Antiform produces garments using reclaimed materials, and sources additional specialist materials and labour from within 20 miles of its studio, based in Leeds (see pages 134–137 for an interview with the founder of Antiform).

Product service systems (PSSs)

An approach that enables a company to offer a mix of products and services rather than provide only products. It is seen as a model for dematerialization since it aims to reduce consumption patterns.

Distribution

5.6

Many cities and rural areas possess a creative fashion and textiles community that contributes to the vitality and identity of the local culture. Although many of these communities have struggled to survive, others are flourishing through a renewed interest in craftsmanship and traditional skills. These creative communities are typically made up of small-scale makers and producers, often associated with the luxury or high-fashion sectors of the industry. They directly or indirectly promote new methods of social engagement since they operate at a local level, but are engaged at a global level, sharing information and experiences with other international communities.

It is usually possible to find a community of artisans in your local area who are willing to work with new designers. By connecting with the people in your creative community, you can find local embroiderers, screen printers, digital printers, textile designers and even small producers or manufacturers willing to support you in your design work.

Moreover, by being involved in a local system of artisans and producers, you are well positioned to reduce some of the negative environmental impacts that are usually associated with large-scale production, including transportation, advertising and marketing, as you will be in a position to sell directly to your local consumers.

You may then be able to redirect money saved into paying fair wages, installing resource-efficient technologies and funding better quality materials.

In addition, you will begin to develop a network for sharing knowledge between suppliers, producers, service providers and consumers. From within this network, sustainable design strategies can be promoted and new ways of engaging with sustainability can be explored. People will begin to share new ideas and experiences and start to develop new ways of engaging with fashion that can bring about a change in the behaviour of everyone involved in the production and consumption of clothing.

5.7

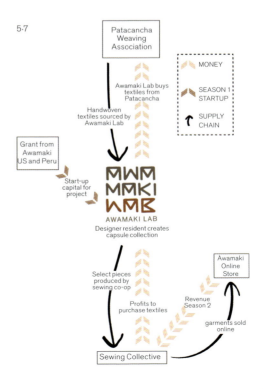

5.8

5.9

5.7–5.10 | Awamaki LAB AW12.

The not-for-profit organization
Awamaki, based in Peru, manages
weaving, knitting and sewing
cooperatives and provides training
and market access to the women in
the cooperatives. Fashion collections
are developed in collaboration with
young designers, and these in turn
provide financial support for the
weavers and the sewing cooperative.

5.10

Isabell de Hillerin

5.11

5.12

In 2009, German designer Isabell de Hillerin set up her own fashion label in Berlin. Working with artisans and manufacturers based in Romania and Moldova, de Hillerin brings traditional weaving and embroidery techniques into contemporary fashion as a way of supporting and protecting regional materials and crafts.

What first inspired you to bring sustainability into your fashion collections?

There is a common thread in all my collections: traditional handmade fabrics and embroidery from Romania and Moldova. These unique materials became an important part of the identity of 'Isabell de Hillerin'. The idea is to strengthen this traditional artisan industry, to work with local manufacturers and to support the production of handmade materials by implementing their cultural skills in a modern fashion context. Apart from that, everything is produced in Germany.

5.11 | Isabell de Hillerin.

5.12 and 5.13 | SS13 collection from Isabell de Hillerin.

Isabelle de Hillerin works with local manufacturers to support the production of handmade materials. Her designs blend tradtional crafts with contemporary design details and at the same time help to publicize the cultural skills of highly skilled craftspeople.

Distribution

5.13

Isabell de Hillerin

5.14

5.15

Why is the preservation of traditional crafts important to you?

All the patterns and materials I saw in my childhood and on visits to Romania left an impression, and by the time I made my final project at the fashion design school in Barcelona, I couldn´t find these beautiful fabrics any more. That was the moment I realized that this unique art of weaving had almost disappeared.

In summer 2008, I made a road trip through Romania and actually found some manufacturers still crafting these folkloric fabrics. These values and skills have to be preserved in some way, so that's why I started in the first place, with the idea of capturing these handmade elements and translating them into my designs. These collaborations are the part I love most about my work and are also a connection to my roots.

5.16

5.14–5.16 | SS13 collection from Isabell de Hillerin.

Isabell worked with women in Moldova and introduced handmade embroidery and other traditional techniques into the collection.

You work with craftspeople in Romania and Moldova; have there been any difficulties in working with people who are traditionally seen as being outside the fashion industry?

Of course, there have been some difficulties. One example is shipment to Moldova. The women I am working with are living in little villages and normally don't have a normal address with a street and house number. So it's not so easy to send them something and explain to the courier I need them to deliver a package without having a real address. But I have the advantage of speaking Romanian, so communication works pretty well, and I can say that even if they don't know what the fashion industry is all about, their interest and passion is incredible.

Do you have any tips or advice for a fashion student who may want to produce a sustainable fashion collection?

Go for it! Of course, there is a large amount of research and hard work behind every collection, but you can feel and see the difference of the quality. In the end, it pays off.

This section focuses on reducing and avoiding the impacts associated with the journey of a garment from the factory floor to the consumer. Although energy and fuel are required for the transportation, storage and distribution of products to the point of sale, retail stores also need energy for lighting and heating. At the same time, garments need protective packing and bundling for easier transportation and storage.

However, it is the volume of products being moved within this system that raises concern, since it is based largely upon predictive sales. Retail buyers anticipate the demand for garments and then estimate the quantities required, which often leads to a problem of overproduction. This means that resources are wasted in production and fossil fuels are used for the needless transportation of surplus stock.

5.17

5.17 and 5.18 | D.dress software from Continuum.

Using the D.dress software from Continuum, you can draw your own dress and see it as a three-dimensional model before the final garment pattern is exported for manufacturing to your own measurements.

Crowdsourcing

Gaining ideas, opinions and services from a large group of people, typically through the Internet.

Distribution

5.18

On-demand production

The overproduction of garments can be avoided in a number of ways, but most recently, advances in new technology have enabled a number of fashion labels and brands to produce garments on demand. Consumers can place personalized orders directly with the supplier, using web-based technology that allows for product customization.

Moreover, digital and web-based technology is dramatically changing the way in which fashion garments are being created. The experimental fashion label Continuum allows consumers to engage in the design process itself by using crowdsourcing web-based technology, which enables them to create their own garments to size and see them in a three-dimensional form online before ordering. Furthermore, consumers can share their ideas and creations with the wider community by connecting with a network of users using Continuum's Internet service.

Each example of this approach relies on providing consumers with the opportunity to participate in the innovation process for a range of new products that extends from jeans to trainers. However, this is taken one step further with the use of 'open-source' websites that allow consumers to download paper patterns so that they can produce garments in their own homes. Rather than transporting goods, the open-source websites promote the notion of transporting information.

DIY fashion

The Internet has provided a valuable platform for small labels and producers to link with consumers. While some labels have developed their own online stores, others promote and sell their products through specialist online retailers. Companies such as Etsy are establishing online communities that extend beyond the marketplace to connect consumers with producers, thinkers, activists and others. Consumers are invited to share ideas, participate in events and learn new skills that support a DIY approach to fashion-making.

This approach to retailing has helped raise the profile of many small fashion producers, bringing in new business without the need for a large financial investment. Although goods still require transporting, which should not be ignored, valuable resources are not wasted, and operations can remain lean since much of the production is conducted to order.

5.19

5.20

5.19 | The 'Homemade Line' from SANS.

Sewing patterns for garments from the 'Homemade Line' by New York-based fashion label SANS can be downloaded from the Internet so that wearers can make the garments at home.

5.20 | Garments by DIY Couture.

Inexperienced sewers can buy simple garment-making instructions online at the DIY Couture website so that they can make their own clothes. By following the step-by-step process, which uses simple visual diagrams, the company aims to help sewing fashion become accessible.

Distribution

Responding to wearers' needs

You do not, however, have to rely upon technology to act as the facilitator between yourself and your consumers in order to develop an innovative approach to fashion. A number of unique fashion labels are exploring product and/or service business combinations. While this can be achieved using web-based technology as previously discussed, it can also work well within a small-scale context where designers engage with their consumers and have the opportunity to respond to specific requests. Moreover, new business models can offer a garment remodelling service, while garments, particularly luxury items, can also be hired or leased rather than owned.

5.21 | Anatomy Vintage store on Etsy.
More than an online retailer, Etsy provides a platform for new designers and labels while bringing together consumers, producers, artists and makers who form a online/offline community.

5.21

An industry often seen as exclusive rather than inclusive, fashion has struggled on a practical level to respond to the needs of many people within society, including wearers with disabilities and/or health concerns, those suffering financial hardship, those with specific religious needs and the ageing population. In fashion magazines and retail stores around the world, consumers are being bombarded with the latest collections and the season's new 'must-have' garments and looks. But while we may aspire to own these products, they are not accessible or essential to everyone.

Developing fashion that essentially meets a need offers the potential to reduce the overproduction of unnecessary products. Responding to actual needs rather than market 'wants' positively reduces the material and natural resources used in both production and distribution. But a genuine need has to be considered more broadly than addressing the practical needs of wearers. While practicality and usability are valued needs, people also need fashion that can, for example, engender emotional well-being, encourage independence and provide security. Few fashion garments generate all of these qualities, but designers have the opportunity to fill real human needs that are sometimes overlooked in the fashion industry.

A number of steps must be considered when designing to meet a need. First, the nature of the need must be established – what are you aiming to address? Next, you have to determine how you can meet the need through the garment's design, and how you will ensure that you have met your aims. It is important to evaluate your work to determine how well you have responded to the need. Do you think you have achieved your objectives? Is the design fit for purpose, or do you need to make further improvements?

5.22

5.23

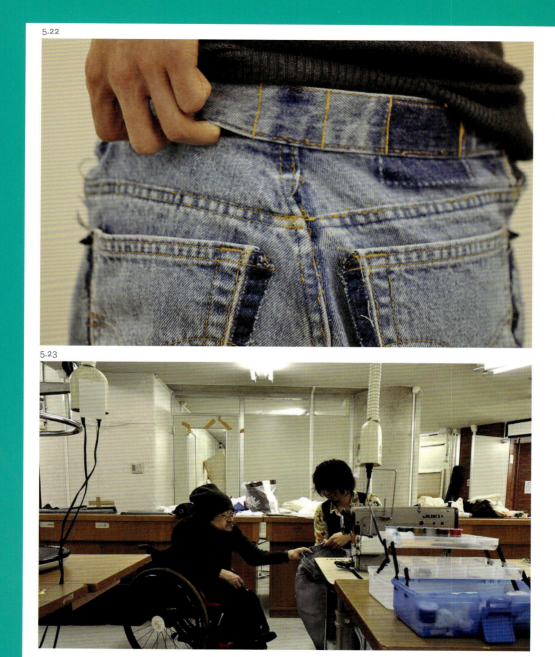

5.22 and 5.23 | Inclusive fashion workshop held at Kyoto University of Art and Design.

Dr Daijiro Mizuno's Inclusive Fashion Workshop was held at Kyoto University of Art and Design after design ethnography (conducted by the author), to explore the balance between the use and look of garments. Designing with people with various impairments as lead users, garments were developed for mutliple uses.

Designing for inclusive fashion

In this design exercise, you will develop a coat that can be worn by a range of people who have difficulties with dexterity and/or movement.

Begin by choosing either menswear or womenswear, and gather together research on trends and fabrics for the next AW season. Next, explore the problems facing users with dexterity and movement issues. If possible, interview people who have dexterity or movement problems and observe participants putting on/taking off and using a coat. Refer back to the instructions in Chapter 3 on 'Designing for empathy' for methods of working with users. Further information can also be found at the Designing with People website at <http://designingwithpeople.rca.ac.uk/methods>.

You will need to find out what different levels and capabilities of use will be encountered, and how these need to be considered in the design of your coat. Problems with movement may include difficulty in reaching or in stretching the arms out, while dexterity issues may involve difficulty with grasping, pinching or pulling objects. For more information on capabilities of use, see the Inclusive Design Toolkit at <www.inclusivedesigntoolkit.com/betterdesign2/>.

As you begin to develop your designs, remember to reflect on your ideas and see if you can find a way to make your garment accessible to a wider community of wearers. Do your designs hinder or alleviate problems with use? Could a variety of people with a range of different needs wear your garments? Although you can design a garment for a specific need, consider how you can reach a wider number of people by thinking through the possible barriers to use. For example, fiddly buttons or the awkward placement of a zipper or pocket can be potential problems for people with dexterity or joint mobility issues.

5.24

5.25

5.24–5.26 | The 'Thais' dress by Xeni.

Specialist fashion label Xeni produces garments for wheelchair users and consumers who have other dexterity or mobility issues. While function is a primary concern, the label is focused towards fashion.

5.26

A garment's use phase – where most of its environmental impacts are created – can be broken down into various activities: wearing, laundering, storing, repairing, adaption and alteration. By gathering information on how people use your garments, you can reveal good as well as poor practices, and see where improvements can be made. You can then begin to encourage improved patterns of use to extend garments' life cycles. This chapter focuses on activities within the use phase, and introduces sustainable design strategies to consider at the outset of the design process.

'Buy less, choose well, make it last.'
Dame Vivienne Westwood

6.1 | A garment from Emma Dulcie Rigby's 'Energy Water Fashion' project.

UK designer Emma Dulcie Rigby has produced a range of garments that incorporate accessible care instructions into the design of the garment.

6

Do not machine wash. Sponge clean with cold water. Avoid alcohol-based products, fabric softeners and solvent cleaners. Never use soaps or detergents. Line dry. Regular reproofing will maintain durable qualities of the fabric and prolong garment life.

6.2

This section focuses on the laundering process, including washing, drying and ironing clothes. Although labelling can play an important part, many people learn how to look after clothing from members of their family. A mother, grandmother or other relative may demonstrate how to use a washing machine, provide advice on stain removal or give tips on ironing delicate fabrics. For other people, laundering can be a bewildering activity learnt by trial and error. The following sections take a look at how we wash, dry, iron and store clothing.

6.2 | Ethical fashion designer Ada Zanditon.

Ada Zanditon is the wear-and-care expert for the environmental cleaning product company Ecover. Zanditon and Ecover work together to promote environmental laundering products and practices.

Washing garments

When washing garments, we use chemically enriched detergents in a washing machine that uses large amounts of water and energy. While this process contributes to the pollution in our waterways, burns fossil fuels and creates CO_2 emissions, little thought is given to the damage it causes our environment.

Our need to wash clothing comes from our personal standards of cleanliness, which relate to sweat and skin contact. Clothes are washed because they are considered 'dirty', but there is little agreement on what this constitutes. Some wearers may wash a garment after one brief wearing, while for others it may be after one or two days of wearing, but this can vary according to what type of clothing is being washed. Sports wear or work wear is frequently viewed as the dirtiest clothing and is repeatedly washed at a much higher temperature than other articles. Meanwhile, clothes such as jumpers and other items that are used for a shorter period are often said to require 'freshening up'.

By understanding the relationship between types or levels of dirt and the appropriate laundering treatments, it is possible to decide whether clothes need a full wash or just a 'rinse'. This highlights the issue that, in general terms, wearers do not think, or possibly know, that the care requirements for a garment are usually determined according to fabric type rather than levels or types of dirt.

The dry-cleaning process

The dry-cleaning process involves cleaning with chemicals rather than water. It has traditionally included using large amounts of the solvent perchloroethylene, or 'Perc'. This chemical is classified as a 'volatile organic compound', or VOC, and is considered to pose a health risk to both humans and animals when it is released in air, water or food. People who briefly come into air contact with Perc may suffer from dizziness, lightheadedness or headaches, but those who work with the chemical on a daily basis have increased health risks, possibly leading to specific forms of cancer.

The dry-cleaning industry is responding to tighter regulations that are restricting the use of Perc, and new developments are leading to cleaner, greener methods. This includes the technique of 'wet cleaning', which uses water in place of solvents in combination with a special programmable, slow-rotating washer and dryer.

You can read more about Perc on the Environmental Protection Agency website: <www.epa.gov/oppt/existingchemicals/ pubs/perchloroethylene_fact_sheet.html>.

Drying and ironing garments

Within most developed societies, the tumble dryer is perceived as a device for convenience. Beyond concerns relating to the amount of energy that is used to operate a tumble dryer, wearers do not typically think about other negative impacts that are incurred when using a dryer. For example, the life cycle of fabrics used in fashion clothing can be reduced by artificial drying methods, and human error can lead the wearer to dry clothing at excessively high temperatures, which can cause shrinkage or distortion. This is apparent when wearers ignore or do not see the care instructions provided by manufacturers relating to the requirements of a specific fibre type.

Equally, it could be argued that ironing can reduce the life cycle of clothing. Irons can be set at an incorrect temperature, steam features can be used unnecessarily, and fabric damage can occur from misuse. The issues surrounding ironing, rather like those of tumble drying, are often made worse by the complex composition of fabrics and their reaction to incorrect temperatures.

Storing clothes

Looking after clothing also includes considering how it will be stored during periods of regular and infrequent use. Fortunately, there seems to be a wealth of advice and information available within general housekeeping books, magazines and websites, as well as specific product information found on many good fashion company websites. However, rather than expecting the wearer to visit websites or read books, perhaps you can find a way to inform your consumers of specific best practice methods. If you understand the requirements needed to keep your garments in good condition, ranging from where garments should be stored to the types of hanger that are best to use, you can inform the wearer of techniques that will keep their garments in better shape.

6.3

6.3 | Hand-knitted sweater by Emma Dulcie Rigby.

The pieces from Emma Duclie Rigby's 'Energy Water Fashion' project were hand knitted from 100 per cent Wensleydale wool and feature accessible care instructions as part of the design.

6.4

6.4 | Oxfam's Vintage Care Guide.

The charity Oxfam (UK) has produced an information guide to support the care of vintage clothing. It provides tips and advice on washing, ironing and general care for a range of different fabric types.

6.5

Disposable fashion

This concept could be explored further in new garment design by creating detachable pieces that are developed to be disposable and biodegradable, which completely eliminates the need for washing. This is becoming a possibility as new technological processes are enabling designers to transform the original properties of a fabric. There are exciting possibilities, too, for recyclable non-woven fabrics, which do not require washing, to be applied within fashion.

Laser-cutting can be used to achieve a lace effect in a non-woven garment that has been joined using ultrasonic bonding techniques. This provides delicacy and ventilation and facilitates recycling, which is a useful approach for single-occasion wear where recycling or composting an item is preferable to laundering it. But you need to think through the impacts of any possible changes at the outset of design, to see if new negative impacts will arise elsewhere in the life cycle of the garment.

While on first appearance it may seem reasonable to make the wearer responsible for improved and safer laundering practices, it is clear that you can be engaging with strategies that can help wearers better manage the care of their garments. You can and should try to find a way to communicate care information to your consumer. Be aware, however, that the information needs to remain accessible and that supplementary material, such as tags and labels, often end up separated from the garment. You need to look for creative techniques to enable the information to stay with the garment, and this can begin with the development of a unique approach to product labelling.

6.5 | Printed paper dress from the 1960s.
The concept of the recyclable paper garment is not a new idea. In the 1960s the boldly patterned paper dress briefly became an icon for instant, disposable fashion.

Disposable clothing

Disposable clothing is traditionally associated with personal protection and isolation, and is used in environments such as the food, medical and health-care industries. The clothing is usually made from a non-woven polypropylene textile, which can be mechanically recycled and used to form other products. Although a non-woven textile is typically not used alone in the production of fashion garments, different non-woven fabrics offer specific functions. This includes fabrics that are liquid repellent and/or fabrics that may be recycled, which can minimize or avoid the need for washing.

6.6

6.7

6.6 and 6.7 | Tyvek dresses by Sukiennik Agnieszka.
The art dresses from Polish designer, Sukiennik Agnieszka
are constructed from Tyvek, a lightweight paper-like
material from DuPont, which can be recycled after use.

Although it is, of course, often necessary to wash clothing, items are sometimes washed purely as a matter of routine. In the earlier sections, we looked at why and how people may wash clothing, but you can take a lead in challenging and altering laundering routines by using creative strategies in your garment design. At the very outset of the design process, you can reflect on the design of a garment to see if it is possible to encourage people to launder less, or not at all, and to use other methods as an alternative to washing.

During the design phase, you can reflect upon your choice of fabrics, textile features and decorative details to see if these selections can help minimize or avoid some of the environmental impacts of laundering. You can select fabrics for their easy-care properties, including fabrics that can be washed, dried and ironed at low temperatures. Alternatively, you can use complex textile patterns or engineered prints that allow stains to blend, delaying the need for washing. This is a particularly useful strategy for cuffs, collars and other high-wear areas within a garment.

It is useful to consider the temporary removal of high-wear components from within a garment, so that only the cuff and collars, for example, are washed, rather than the whole garment. The ability to separate garment sections, either through a modular system or by simple separation of one component from another, allows the wearer to reduce the need for a full garment wash. Pieces that can be removed can then be treated specifically and appropriately, allowing the wearer to spot-treat stains or freshen up sections without the need for a full garment wash.

6.8

6.9

6.8 | 'Fragment' textiles by Refinity and Berber Soepboer.

Fioen van Balgoo and Beber Soepboer collaborated to develop garments which use shaped modular pieces that can be 'clicked and folded' together to form many different configurations.

6.9 | 'The Magnificent Seven' collection by Bruno Kleist.

Danish-based designer Bruno Kleist has developed a menswear collection using natural techniques including fungus-dyeing and rust-dyed prints. The collection was created to reflect decay and transformation, which at the same time deflects attention away from stains and marks collected through use.

In contemporary Western society, most wearers do not typically engage in repairing worn or damaged clothing. There is very little evidence of repair work being done as a regular activity, except perhaps for sewing on buttons and fixing hems. This lack of engagement may be due to a number of factors including a shortage of household skills, the attraction of new and relatively cheap clothing, the price of repair compared with that of new clothes, and the availability of repair services. The next sections take a look at how you can motivate wearers to engage in repair and alteration.

6.10

6.10 | Woolfiller by Heleen Klopper.

Woolfiller, from Netherlands-based designer Heleen Klopper, can be used to hide stains and fill holes in woollen garments. Woolfiller can be applied by hand without the need for complex equipment and will remain fixed even after washing.

6.11–6.13 | Wearable repair kits by Sara McBeen.

Californian product designer Sara McBeen has redesigned the sewing repair kit into a portable and wearable object, which is decorative and easily accessible to the wearer.

Repairing garments

Initially, for economic reasons, clothes were carefully maintained and repaired because labour was cheap compared with the cost of materials and new garments. Unfortunately, the task of repairing and altering clothes at home and in industry has almost disappeared within two generations.

In repairing a garment, you are proposing to restore a damaged or decaying item to a good or sound condition. With clothing, there are many techniques for repair, including darning, patching and appliqué, all of which can mend or hide a repair. You may be able to encourage wearers to repair clothing, either at home or professionally, but you will have to consider how the work will be carried out and by whom. Can you support the wearer to undertake the repair work? Or will you advise that the wearer seeks specialist assistance? What methods of repair might be used?

One of the biggest challenges is encouraging people to wear garments that have been repaired, particularly if the repair is visible. Historically, wearing repaired clothing was a signifier of financial hardship, so it has been, and perhaps still is, socially unacceptable to wear visibly repaired clothing. You can begin to shift this view by encouraging an individual to wear their repairs as a symbol of distinction and individuality. You can encourage the wearer to celebrate stains, holes and tears by enhancing and enriching these 'new motifs' using decorative techniques, which could be executed in very different ways by both novices and experienced repairers.

6.11

6.12

6.13

Altering and adapting garments

A growing movement within sustainable fashion has been reviving the use of craft skills. Aside from creative approaches to repair, these forums promote other techniques including the practice of altering clothing to upgrade garments that might otherwise be discarded.

In altering a garment, the aim is to make it appear different. Alterations may be slight, for example, changing a long-sleeve shirt to a short-sleeve shirt, or so significant that the original appearance of the garment almost completely disappears.

During the design phase, you can build in strategies enabling wearers to adapt the garment either temporarily or permanently at a later stage. For example, you may develop a garment so that it intentionally transforms during use, moving between one form and another. Alternatively, you may provide the wearer with the relevant information and materials to transform the garment themselves. In some cases, you will not be able to influence alteration since another service provider may take this on (see Chapter 7). But if you would like to prepare a garment for alteration, it is important to establish at what point in its life cycle it might be transformed.

6.14

6.15

6.14 and 6.15 | Fernando Brizio's 'Restarted' dress.

The colourful patterns on Fernando Brizio's dresses are created using felt tip pens. The patterns can be removed by washing, leaving the owner with a blank canvas on which to create a new pattern.

Use

6.16

Design for garment ageing

As you begin to design a garment and select materials, techniques and processes, it is useful to consider how the component parts of the garment will age during wear. You can then look for opportunities to exploit particular characteristics that may enable you to extend its life cycle.

For example, many fabrics eventually develop holes through excessive wear; unless repaired, these will grow as the garment is repeatedly washed and worn. However, you can exploit this by constructing a garment using two layers of fabric with specific features sandwiched between the layers. As the garment is washed and worn, and the holes and tears spread, these new attributes are revealed. This presents the negative ageing qualities of a fabric as a positive feature in the garment's design, bringing out new value-added qualities while avoiding the need for repair.

6.16 | 'Let's Get Lost' skirt, bustier and jacket by Lisa Hawthorne.

Chelsea College of Art and Design MA Textiles graduate Lisa Hawthorne has developed a range of textiles that are designed to reveal embellishment details as the garment ages. As the natural fabrics wear, the embellishments that are buried in the fabrics begin to appear.

As an alternative to preparing garments for ageing, a range of methods can be explored to encourage wearers to engage in repair work. However, you need to provide them with appropriate information to support this. If you wish to encourage the wearer to seek professional assistance, you may have to provide a list of recommended service providers.

In fashion history, there are many examples of modularity that can become a reference point for new fashion design ideas. For example, during the mid-seventeenth century, it became fashionable for women to wear 'the stays', a corseted bodice worn as an undergarment. The stays could be worn with sleeves that were detached and reattached using decorative ribbons so that the wearer could change the appearance and function of the garment according to need.

Detachable features were also applied in menswear when, in the early eighteenth century, it became fashionable to match the pattern used in a waistcoat with the cuffs on a coat. Rather than buy many new coats, the cuffs were designed to be removed and reattached using hooks and eyes, which enabled the cuffs to be washed or replaced separately from the coat.

Alternatively, you may want to support the wearer to actively engage in repairing, which may involve providing additional materials, such as extra fabric and matching threads, along with specific instructions. This can be done more easily if you explore the design of modular garments, which can provide an opportunity to replace or repair one piece of a garment without affecting the rest of the system.

While you can engage with different creative approaches to encourage the wearer to repair their garment, it can be useful for you to identify areas of high wear during production. If you can reinforce these areas, the wearer can get more wear from the garment. Reinforcement can be invisible or visible and/or decorative, and if you would like to take this approach, it may help to read about the technique of 'upcycling' in Chapter 7.

6.17

6.17 | Stays with attached sleeves, from the mid-seventeenth century.

Clothes with removable sections are easier to repair or replace since the damaged pieces can be removed without disrupting the rest of the garment.

6.18

6.18 | Cotton pique jacket with grosgrain collar and cuffs by Christian Dior.

During construction the seams and hem of a haute couture garment are usually left deep so the garment can be altered in the future. If the garment is adapted then the fabric is usually not cut away so that it may be changed on many occasions.

Designing modular garments

Your task is to try to develop a range of detachable features for use with fashion garments that can facilitate replacement or repair. In particular, you should aim to develop a novel and creative attachment system.

Can you find another example of a detachable feature within fashion and dress in historical costume collections? Or can you track down another unique solution to the issue of repair? What makes this new solution interesting?

Who do you think would have been responsible for undertaking the repair work, and what resources and skills do you think were needed to complete the work? Can you apply this technique in the design of a new fashion collection?

6.19 and 6.20 | Bob and John interchangeable knitwear.

Nottingham Trent University MA graduate Jonie Worton wants wearers to interact and connect with her garments by choosing sleeves to suit different contexts.

6.19

6.20

Lizzie Harrison

6.21

6.22

Lizzie Harrison is the founder of the UK fashion company Antiform, which was established in 2007 and produces fashion clothing from recycled and locally sourced materials found in the Yorkshire region. Lizzie set up a partner company, ReMade in Leeds, to provide workshops, repairs, clothes exchanges and other events for the local community. Lizzie gives lectures and talks on sustainable fashion and works with many organizations, designers and researchers.

6.21 | Lizzie Harrison.

6.22 | ReMade in Leeds sewing workshop.

Under the in-house brand of Antiform, ReMade in Leeds offers sewing workshops designed to help wearers get the most out of their garments. Wearers can learn skills such as upcycling, garment repair and alteration techniques.

What was the vision for the brand when you started the boutique and label, and was sustainability important to you then?

Sustainability has always been core to my work – the way I approach my work reflects the values I hold in all areas of my life. As a designer, I only want to produce pieces in a responsible way. When I started the brand, I was working in Leeds as a production manager and running community workshops, and I realized how much waste textile there is in the UK fashion industry and how many skilled makers there are within the local area. It was this active exploration that led me to the idea of setting up a brand with a local supply chain.

The vision for the brand was to produce fashion locally and explore, first, what this would look like aesthetically, and also what other opportunities this would create in terms of services we could offer.

6.23 | Antiform SS13.

In your Antiform collections, you make new garments from local and/or reclaimed materials using techniques such as upcycling. Why?

We use materials we can source locally to our studio in Leeds, Yorkshire. When I started researching, there were two really key local materials sources: first, the waste textiles we all generate when we 'throw away' our old clothing, especially garments that are not suitable for resale through charity shops; and second, local textiles producers and their factory waste.

Starting the brand in Yorkshire, with its long textiles history, really shaped how we sourced. We now work with predominantly wool tweeds, suiting, cotton and polycotton jerseys and knitted wools.

Upcycling has given us the freedom to take materials that are currently considered 'waste' and therefore have a low value, and, through craftsmanship, turn them into valuable fashion pieces.

You run a variety of sewing workshops that help people learn how to alter, upcycle or repair clothes. Is it important for you to educate your consumer?

When I started Antiform, which was partly driven by a desire to reduce the textiles waste the industry was producing, I felt there was a bit of a conflict in my ideas – on one hand wanting to reduce textiles waste, and on the other setting up a business that was producing products. This made me want to really rethink what a fashion brand does, so running fashion workshops with our customers made sense.

6.23

Lizzie Harrison

You run a fashion label and a boutique, as well as give workshops and get involved in other projects. What have been the benefits of running such a diverse business?

Running such a diverse business is really exciting. Fashion is changing, and the world is changing. Climate change and water and oil scarcity are going to keep bringing changes over the coming years. I am really interested in how small business can create dynamic business models to become sustainable and breed sustainability. One of the benefits of being a small organization that is not dependent on growth-led economic models is that you gain flexibility, which is definitely a commercial advantage. All the activities we run feed into the same desire to produce responsible clothing and change the way customers consume, use and dispose of fashion.

Do you have any advice or tips for emerging fashion designers who may want to look at developing a business that makes new garments and also offers services?

I think we are going to see more and more diversification from fashion brands. This is really exciting because it unlinks 'fashion consumption' from resource use and allows consumers to buy into a brand without having to buy a physical product.

My advice is to really explore your market and understand your customers' needs. This will give you a great insight into how they use clothing and how you, as a brand, might participate in services with the customer. Trialling services with our own customers is something we do extensively before we launch anything and is great as it gives us plenty of feedback.

What is your vision for the brand in the future?

My vision for the future is to carry on pushing the boundaries of fashion, product, retail and service to look for new and emerging opportunities to change customers' perspectives on fashion. An example of this has been our recent use of unused retail shops in city-centre high streets to create a travelling showcase of the best products made in Leeds.

Ultimately, the aim is to continue to deliver sustainable fashion and services that seamlessly fit with the values and needs of our customers.

6.24

6.25

6.24 and 6.25 | Antiform SS13.

Antiform garments are created using reclaimed materials. All of the materials and resources involved in the production of the garments are sourced within 20 miles of the design studio in Leeds, Yorkshire.

Garments are thrown away for many reasons: they may be worn out or unfashionable, may no longer fit, or may just not look good. Although more textiles are being collected for recycling, clothing is still discarded alongside general household waste. The increased circulation of low-value, poor-quality products has also reduced the capacity for reuse. This chapter explores how approaches to reuse, remanufacturing and recycling are opening up a new range of creative possibilities to minimize waste. Moreover, it highlights the barriers to improved reuse and recycling schemes, which could be challenged to encourage a drive for change.

'The recycling of textiles into upcycled garments is what makes us sustainable. We create style that outlasts seasons while still managing to retain the original ethos of individuality off the peg.'
Annika Sanders and Kerry Seager, founders of Junky Styling

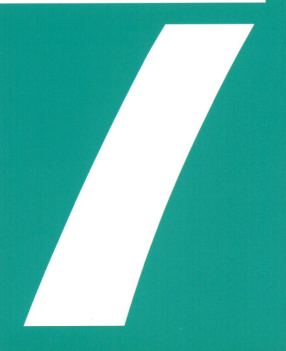

7.1 | A coat from Karen Jessen's Benu-Berlin collection, 2012.

Karen Jessen, a graduate from the MA program at ESMOD Berlin, developed her collection by combining craftsmanship with the recycled materials from 70 pairs of jeans, 200 T-shirts and three discarded leather sofas.

7

Garments are reused in many ways, depending on their condition and the opportunities available to the wearer. A garment can be passed among family members, or exchanged or resold through a second-hand or vintage retailer. It can be donated or sold to a third-party organization, such as a charity, which can resell it, export it or send it for material recycling. Moreover, new fashion labels have emerged that specialize in developing new garments created from existing garments, remnant stock or surplus materials.

7.2

7.2 | Eva Zingoni RTW Season 4 collection.

With a background in couture, designer Eva Zingoni uses recycled and surplus luxury fabrics gathered from the Paris fashion houses for her limited edition range.

Reusing fashion garments

One of the most well-known routes for reuse is passing the item to charity. Many charitable and voluntary organizations worldwide redistribute discarded clothing to be sold in local or national stores, or sent overseas to other distributors. Wearers drop garments into a clothing bank or second-hand store, or use a kerbside collection system. The items are then categorized by grade at a sorting centre. The highest grade are those garments considered best for resale in national stores. Other main categories include garments suitable for export, for recycling into rags and wipers; and for material recycling. Unfortunately, some garments are deemed unsuitable for all of these and will be sent to landfill or incinerated.

7.3

Designing for reuse

The reuse market currently sits alongside a recycling system including the development of new materials spun from a mix of shredded pre- and post-consumer textile waste. While these services are complementary, fashion history tells us that clothing reuse can be an efficient method for reducing waste. With this in mind, you can begin to design garments for reuse until they have gone beyond repair.

Although the value attributed to cloth means that a garment can be recycled for its materials, this relies on the quality and suitability of the fabric. The problem is that the availability of good-quality garments suitable for reuse is outweighed by large volumes of poor-quality products.

7.4

Retailer swap schemes

There has been a growth in the online sale or exchange of garments through retailers such as eBay and Gumtree, which have helped increase the flow and accessibility of second-hand clothing. Moreover, there has been a rise in the popularity of exchange events and websites, and a number of retailer swap schemes are now in operation. In association with the charity Oxfam, Marks and Spencer began its 'Shwopping' campaign in 2012, to encourage consumers to visit M&S stores to donate clothing to Oxfam for reuse or remodelling before being sold in the charity's stores.

While these schemes raise awareness of the benefits of reuse, the number of items donated is not as significant as we would think. Statistics reveal that although there has been an increase in donated garments, greater improvement lies in direct reuse between family and friends, which is on the decline. How would you encourage wearers to pass on unwanted garments to a friend?

7.3 | Surplus materials project by Esther Lui Po.

From the Hong Kong Design Institute, student Esther Lui Po Chu has creatively woven together surplus fashion labels gathered from clothing manufacturers.

7.4 | Striped sweatsuit by Kathrine Gram Hvejsel.

A reuse/redesign MA student competition at the Kolding School of Design, Denmark was run in conjunction with H&M Denmark and The Red Cross. The winning student collection was by Kathrine Gram Hvejsel.

7.5

Remanufacturing existing materials

During the design phase, designers often choose materials for aesthetic and functional reasons, but you can explore the concept of developing a new garment by reworking existing clothing or working with unwanted stock and/or surplus materials.

The reclaimed fabrics used to remanufacture garments can come from pre-consumer and post-consumer waste. Pre-consumer waste is the refuse material generated during the manufacture of textile products, while post-consumer waste is thought of as pre-worn, manufactured garments that are sourced through second-hand clothing merchants and charities. By using these resources, you can remanufacture existing garments, fragments or lengths of cloth to create new garments.

7.5 and 7.6 | Limited edition garments by Christopher Raeburn for the Remade in Switzerland collection.

Christoper Raeburn collaborated with Swiss manufacturer Victorinox to create the 'Remade in Switzerland' limited edition collection that was manufactured from surplus Swiss military stock, including parachutes.

7.6

7.7

While this process is successful when making one garment, it is often challenging when you want to achieve a standardized fashion garment or collection. When working with reclaimed materials, it becomes difficult to reproduce one garment into a repeated set or series because the material supplies are irregular and the quantities unpredictable – so you need to consider this at the start of your design process.

You will also need to consider any technical constraints that may impinge on your production process. For example, if you are remanufacturing an existing garment, you need to be mindful of the condition of the raw materials, noting stains, holes or areas of fraying or discoloration, and working around or with these traits.

You will also have to work out a method for the careful deconstruction of existing garments so that you have enough workable fabric to use. While the deconstruction of one garment may be manageable, it can be much more time-consuming when you are deconstructing ten or more garments. In addition, you will have to source a large enough quantity of garments to use, which may be difficult and/or costly. For some designers, these issues may seem too complex or difficult to take on board as a workable or worthwhile approach, but others find that these perceived difficulties act as a catalyst for new fashion ideas.

7.7 | Esprit fabric waste collection by Wister Tsang, 2012.

Wister Tsang was the 2012 EcoChic Design Award Hong Kong winner. Tsang's collection was constructed using production fabric waste from the fashion company Esprit.

Co-designed fashion

The strategy of upcycling has seen a growth in new business opportunities for smaller fashion labels in recent years. These producers are able to offer unique and personalized services that enable wearers to engage in the creative process.

Although you may be happy to consult with wearers at the initial stage of the design process, you may want to work much more closely with your wearer in a co-designing situation. By working together as a team with the designer, the wearer is able to have a greater input into how the garment is refurbished or remanufactured.

You can also prepare wearers to undertake their own upcycling projects by providing customization packs with your garments; wearers are then placed in the position of determining their own creative choices. Essentially, the point remains that value must be added to the material or garment, regardless of whether the technique used to upcycle employs, for example, stitching, appliqué, printing and/or embroidery.

7.8

7.9

7.10

7.11

7.12

7.8 and 7.9 | A customized jacket by Queenie and Ted.

Based in East London, Queenie and Ted upcycle discarded, good-quality garments through appliqué, using quirky crafted motifs that can be personalized when commissioned by the customer.

7.10–7.12 | 'Make Do and Mend' workshop.

Participants creatively mend damaged clothes in the 'Make Do and Mend' project workshops led by the author and a team of researchers at Sheffield Hallam University.

'Upcycling' is a term that is used to describe the technique of upgrading and adding value to a product or material that may otherwise be discarded. Rather than recycling, which can result in a downgrading and reduction in value of a material or product, upcycling allows you to increase the worth and value of a material while prolonging its life. The technique can be applied in the design and manufacture of a new garment, or be used to refurbish or remanufacture an existing garment.

Upcycling provides endless opportunities for designers to be creative. You can aim to add value to an existing garment through a small alteration or decorative detail, or you can produce entire garments by creatively using waste offcuts and scraps, or found/existing objects. This idea works particularly well when working with a single item in multiples; for example, you can join together rejected or broken zips in blocks of colour to create bold accessory items. More extreme approaches have included using materials such as newspapers for couture garments, as in the work of UK designer Gary Harvey.

When selecting materials, you will need to take time to prepare them for use, which may involve selecting and collecting the items, washing them and deconstructing the component parts to be used – all of which takes time that will add to the cost price of the finished product. Designing and making upcycled pieces can therefore take considerable time, especially if small runs of products are to be made.

7.13

7.13 | A knitted accessory piece by Andrea da Costa.

Andrea da Costa, a textile design graduate from Central Saint Martins in London, used discarded and sustainable materials, such as surplus tubing, barkcloth and organic felting wool, to produce a unique line of knitted accessory pieces.

7.14

7.15

7.16

7.14 and 7.15 | Upcycled garments by Jennifer Whitty and Holly McQuillan.

Using strategies such as upcycling and zero-waste processes, Jennifer Whitty and Holly McQuillan have reused existing, discarded clothing to create a transformable garment in a pilot project for a corporate uniform manufacturer.

7.16 | 'Patchwork' leather jacket by Martina Spetlova.

Originally from the Czech Republic, designer Martina Spetlova patchworks together offcuts and surplus materials, including zips, jerseys and leather, to create dramatic garment forms.

A personalized approach to upcycling

For this exercise, you are to upcycle an existing, but damaged garment so that it is both appealing and wearable to a specific wearer.

Ask a friend or relative to lend you a garment that is wearable, but has a specific site of damage; for example, it may be either torn or stained. Then, interview the owner about their aesthetic likes and dislikes so you can build a picture of their favourite colours, textures, patterns, decorative details and so on. Develop a mood board that reflects your wearer's aesthetic style.

Next, develop initial design ideas for motifs and patterns that can be used to conceal or enhance the damage. Identify appropriate textile techniques that can help you to achieve your design. Get feedback from your wearer. Which ideas do they like? Do they have any suggestions?

Start to collect together various resources and materials for embellishment, and look for waste and surplus materials that may add creative value to your design.

Choosing one design with your wearer, either work over the top of the damage using the concept of a patch, or work directly on the cloth and embellish around the wear. The intention is to make the garment wearable by adding value through a unique and personalized approach to upcycling.

You can use this approach to create a range of new personalized upcycled pieces that could be manufactured from waste and surplus materials.

7.17

7.17–7.19 | 'T-shirt Hoody' project by Tauko.

Based in Helsinki, the fashion label Tauko will produce custom-made pieces for clients who visit their Kruno studio shop. The company tailored one of their most popular products, the 'Karata' hoody, using a customer's old favourite shirt to add details.

7.18

719

Although recycling uses energy, studies have shown it is better to reuse a material rather than process new raw fibres. This has led to developments enabling fashion designers to use fabrics constructed from reclaimed materials or recycled fibres, some of which are also themselves recyclable. As fashion and textile producers develop relationships with waste management and recycling operators, we may see the emergence of an improved range of fabrics and technologies. In the meantime, designers should look for opportunities to promote and engage with recycling processes and materials.

Textile recycling

While textile recycling can be managed by some charities, typically, a third party buys and collects the unwanted waste from a charity alongside that collected from industry, including household waste such as curtains and bed linen, and industrial textile waste gathered from fashion and textile producers, hotels, hospitals, industrial laundries and local authority agencies.

Damaged garments can be recycled into rags and cleaning cloths, but those considered unsuitable for this will be processed back into fibrous form. During recycling, fibres are separated by chemical or mechanical processes. The separated fibres can then be remanufactured into a new material used to make, for example, acoustic or insulation products. Alternatively, the fibres may be used as padding for mattresses or upholstery. But while this is a good reuse of discarded materials, the original value of the fibre has been downgraded.

7.20

7.20 | The Viva La Vida collection by Carmen Artigas.

This collection of handmade accessories was developed through the El Cereso Prison craft programme in Mexico City. The products are made from 100 per cent recyclable polyethylene.

7.21 | A solar-powered jacket from Zegna Sports.

This jacket from the Zegna Sports label from Ermenegildo Zegna is constructed from recycled plastic materials and incorporates detachable solar panels within the sleeves, which can produce enough energy to charge a mobile phone.

7.21

Working with textiles recyclers

Some of the challenges facing the recycling industry are made worse by poor relationships between fashion and textiles producers and recyclers. Producers are increasingly using blended fibres that are typically downgraded since the fibres cannot be separated. As a producer, you can alleviate this by using mono-materials, as discussed in Chapter 3.

Moreover, it can be difficult for recyclers to separate the components of garments that have undergone complex manufacturing processes. You can help by developing garments that are designed for easier disassembly, preferably using automated systems, as discussed in Chapter 4.

Using recycled materials and fibres

Great strides have recently been made in developing fabrics and yarns from recycled materials. Natural fibres need to be blended with (non-recycled) virgin fibres since the recycling process produces a poorer quality yarn. Although the process of recycling natural fibres remains largely unchanged, there have been advances in the development of recycled synthetic fibres. With processes achievable on a large scale, polymers such as polyethylene terephthalate (PET) have been developed, commonly derived from products like plastic water bottles. Companies such as Patagonia, Marks and Spencer and H&M have been using these fibres to develop products ranging from fleece garments to jeans. Moreover, these fibres are now themselves becoming recyclable. This is discussed further in the case study on closed-loop systems.

The Global Recycle Standard

To check whether claims made about the recycled content of a fabric are valid, look for a Global Recycle Standard (GRS) certification. Administered by the Textile Exchange since 2011, this independent organization aims to verify the amount of recycled content within a fabric, while at the same time expecting producers and suppliers to meet specific standards in relation to environmental and social criteria. Importantly, it places an emphasis on tracking and tracing the product from source to sale, and on producers and suppliers using clear, approved labeling.

<http://textileexchange.org/content/global-recycle-standard>

As outlined in Chapter 2, the term 'closed-loop system' describes the process of consistently reusing a material without allowing it to enter the waste stream. Other terms that may be used include 'circular economy', 'cradle-to-cradle' and 'closed-loop fibre-to-fibre recycling'.

Fibres now seen more often in closed-loop systems of fashion production are those that have developed synthetically. For example, companies such as Patagonia are recycling polyester garments in conjunction with Teijin's 'ECO CIRCLE' fibre-to-fibre recycling system. Chemical recycling technology transforms the polyester textile waste into a new fibre that can be remanufactured into new garments.

The programme is exciting because it allows a fibre to be recycled to an identical or similar quality to the original fibre, even when processing large quantities, which cannot currently be achieved with all fibre types. However, this system of recycling is not readily available, making it difficult to promote as a method for wearers to engage with.

There are, however, other ways to achieve a closed-loop system of production. You can select materials that can be reprocessed to make the same type of material and product (as with polyester), or you can choose materials that are biodegradable or compostable, which are positively contributing to the biosphere while safely decomposing.

7.22

7.23

SHED ME CLOTHES

Clothing that sheds layers to reduce the impact of laundering.

Inspired by the shedding of snake skin.

Water Soluble Yarn

The fabric is made up of several layers, knitted together with water soluble yarn.

PVA (polyvinyl alcohol) yarn is used. PVA is non-toxic, odourless and has a high tensile strength and flexibility. It is fully degradable and a quick dissolver.

Construction:
Made up of several natural fibre fabric layers, stitched together and separated by water soluble yarn.

TOP

UNDER

How:
Spraying the top or under layer with water will cause the liquid to permeate through the fabric to the water soluble yarn. This meeting will cause the water soluble yarn to dissolve, thus the layer will peel away.

TOP

Peeled layers:
The dirty layers that have been peeled away from the garment can be safely disposed of via composting.

End-of-Life

153

7.24

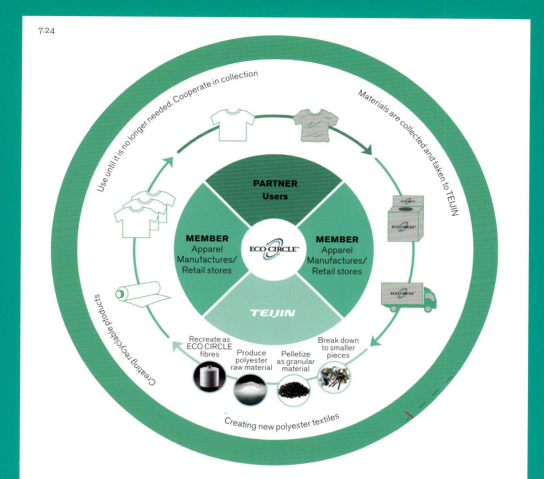

7.22 and 7.23 | Katie Ledger's 'Shed Me Clothes' project.

Katie Ledger has proposed that a fashion garment could be constructed in layers, each layer being composted as it wears away with age.

7.24 | The 'ECO CIRCLE' recycling system from Teijin Fibers in Japan.

Closed-loop production

Moreover, as discussed in Chapter 3, the selected fabric can be enhanced using responsible surface decoration and embellishment techniques. UK designer Kate Goldsworthy has experimented with a wide range of hi-tech tools and textile techniques to expand the creative potential of synthetic fibres without disrupting the material's recycling potential.

Working within a closed-loop system of production also opens up other possibilities, from developing fashion with an extended life cycle to exploring fashion with an ephemeral quality. As new textile developments continue, responsibly produced, disposable, one-off garments become a closer reality. Researcher Suzanne Lee explores the concept of 'biocouture' as a novel response to fashion that is purposely designed not to last. The materials that Lee uses can be safely composted and naturally break down over time.

Growth in the use of recyclable materials is likely to be limited until there have been greater advances in textile recycling systems. However, you should continue to explore these options in readiness for industry improvements in response to consumers' demands to engage with recycling technology.

7.25

7.26

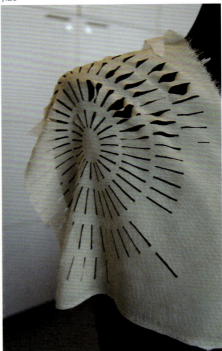

7.25 and 7.26 | Recyclable polyester project.

A concept for a recyclable polyester garment from students (Eva Sofia Aude, Vibe Lindhardt Fælled, Ramona Reile and Petja Zorec) from the Kolding School of Design, Denmark.

7.27

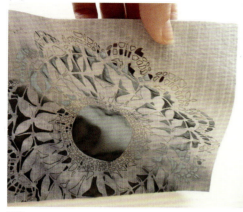

7.28

7.29

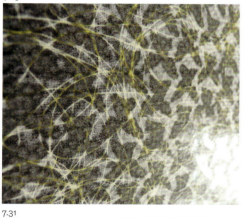

7.30

7.31

7.27–7.31 | 'Mono Finishing' project by Dr Kate Goldsworthy, 2008–2010.

Sustainable fashion researcher Dr. Kate Goldsworthy produced a range of mono-material samples made from 100 per cent polyester. No glues, stitching or finishing chemicals are used and the samples are fully recyclable.

Wayne Hemingway

7.32

7.32–7.34 | McDonald's UK uniform project by Hemingway Design.

Hemingway Design collaborated with Worn Again and UK uniform provider Dimensions for McDonald's UK. The project involved the development of a closed-loop uniform that can be recycled and reprocessed into new products. The uniforms are to be worn by over 85,000 employees.

In the early 1980s, UK designer Wayne Hemingway, with his partner Gerardine, established the Red or Dead fashion label, which went on to win a number of accolades including the British Fashion Council's Street Style Designer of the Year Award in 1996, 1997 and 1998. Now leading the Hemingway Design agency, Hemingway is involved in a number of projects and initiatives driven by sustainable design principles.

What first inspired your interest in sustainability?

I was brought up in a thrifty household long before the word 'sustainability' was used. The house was full of making new from old (long before the word 'upcycling' was coined!), reusing was a mantra, and any form of waste was frowned upon. Thrift is the cornerstone of sustainability. Our days on Camden Market started by selling second-hand clothes, so it's in our blood. But while we are driven by thrift and a hatred of waste, we are also aware that it's the right way to go.

How did the partnership with Worn Again help you in the design of the McDonald's uniform presented at the 2012 Olympic Games?

The project included developing uniforms for 87,500 McDonald's staff, so for us great design usually results when there is a real purpose and focus. The partnership with Worn Again and the drive for 'closed-loop' provided this; technology and design together is very powerful.

End-of-Life

7·33

7·34

Did you encounter any unexpected challenges in the design and production process of the uniforms?

Yes, indeed. The technology for what we are trying to achieve is truly in its infancy and only really resolved in Japan, which is too far away to make use of the Japanese recycling factories. It is making us work very hard to ensure that the UK has the facilities we need.

Do you think enough is being done in the fashion industry to reduce or reuse textile waste?

There is always more that can be done. Perhaps the fashion industry has been slower than some, and vanity can pull a veil over issues, but the industry will catch up.

Do you have any advice or tips for fashion design students who may want to develop a sustainable fashion collection?

Do the detail, make sure that there is no greenwashing, and make sure that the underlying philosophy is clearly communicated without being too over the top. Above all, work hard to ensure that the sustainable elements do not compromise the commerciality – if you don't make money, then all your sustainable principles will evaporate.

So what should you do next? Many strategies can be used to create fashion for sustainability, but if you want to be really engaged, you may need to employ different or new approaches to design that can involve stepping outside traditional conventions. While sustainability is viewed by some as a restriction to innovation, for many designers it is this creative approach to fashion that has led to unique business opportunities.

New types of fashion practice may encourage producers and consumers to see fashion differently. This could help garments to become valuable objects to be cherished and kept, or perhaps hired rather than owned. However, such new practices need you to engage with approaches that encourage wearers to actively participate with fashion garments. If sustainable fashion is to flourish, we have to change the way in which we manufacture and use garments, which needs producers and wearers to share the responsibility for reducing impacts in the life cycle of a garment.

Over the course of this book, you have been introduced to a range of discussions and approaches drawn together to help you reflect on your design practice. While the following pages highlight particular references, books and online resources, you should undertake your own research as a way to build your knowledge and extend your practice. Try to engage with online communities, industry organizations and associations, and library teams, who may be able to direct you towards specific, focused information. This will help you manage your research time efficiently and ensure that you find up-to-date knowledge.

8.1 | Fake Natoo's Reclothing Bank–1 collection.

This full-length dress is made from reclaimed materials as part of designer Na Zhang's Reclothing Bank project.

Artisan
A term used to describe a highly skilled maker or craftsperson who may makes products by hand.

Biodegradable
A material's ability to be ecologically decomposed.

Biofuels
Fuels developed from renewable materials such as bark.

Carbon footprint
The volume of gas emissions measured as a consequence of production and consumption activities.

Closed-loop
A closed-loop production system, or circular economy, aims to eliminate waste through the biological or technical recycling of discarded materials or products.

CO_2 Emissions
Carbon dioxide (CO_2), along with other gases, such as methane, is released into the atmosphere by, for example, burning fossil fuels such as gas, coal and oil.

Corporate social responsibility
A policy developed by a company that sets out its environmental and ethical aims, goals and standards.

Crowdsourcing
Gaining ideas, opinions and services from a large group of people, typically through the Internet.

Design for disassembly
A strategy focused on developing products that can be quickly and easily separated for the reuse and recycling of materials and components.

Design for sustainability
An approach to design that advocates a reduction in the environmental and social impacts arising from production and consumption activities.

Distribution
The transportation of resources and supplies for textile processes and manufacturing services, and the distribution of finished goods to retail markets and warehouses.

Eco or Green fashion
Fashion that focuses on eliminating the environmental impacts associated with the production of a garment.

End-of-life (EOL)
A term used to describe the point at which a product is considered at the end of its useful life and ready for disposal.

Environmental impact
The positive or negative effects on the environment that emerge as a result of production and/or consumption activities.

Ethical fashion
Clothing that is manufactured according to human and labour rights set by the International Labour Organization.

Fair trade
Fair trade products support social developments by paying fair prices for goods and services while reinvesting profit back into the local community.

Human-centred design
Human- or user-centred design refers to a process for developing products that focuses on people's needs and abilities.

Input
The materials, resources and social requirements needed during the life cycle of a garment.

Landfill
A hole in the ground that is filled with waste material and may, when full, be covered and re-landscaped.

Life cycle
All the stages in the life of a product from extraction of raw materials to end-of-life.

Life cycle assessment
The measurable assessment of a product's inputs and outputs (materials and resources) across all stages of the life cycle.

Mono-material
A fabric of a single fibre type.

Non-governmental organization
An organization that may have a social or political agenda, but is set up to run independently of any government institution or for-profit company.

Offshore
Services or supplies provided by a company in a country different from the one where the products are being designed, manufactured or sold.

Organic
In fashion, refers to clothing and textiles made using environmentally friendly processes from field to manufacture.

Output
The material and resource waste and emissions, and the social impacts produced during the life cycle of a garment.

Post-consumer waste
This is textile waste that is created by wearers through the disposal of garments.

Pre-consumer waste
This is textile waste that is created during the production processes of manufacturers and suppliers.

Stakeholder
An individual or group affected by the decisions and activities within a company.

Supply chain
Consists of a network of suppliers and service providers that are needed to manufacture, distribute and sell fashion garments.

Sustainable design strategy
A framed approach that can be employed by a designer to help reduce specific environmental and/or social impacts associated with the production, use and disposal of a product.

Upcycling
A technique of upgrading and adding value to a product or material that may otherwise be discarded.

Users
Refers to the person who may use the product, which in fashion often denotes the wearer.

Virgin fibre
A fibre that has not yet been used in the production of a fabric.

Well-being
This term refers to our mental and/or physical feelings or experiences of and towards life.

Online magazines and networks

Change Observer

A US-based online magazine that includes thoughtful, insightful articles and features on a range of sustainable design topics. Book reviews can help steer you towards new resources.
<http://changeobserver.designobserver.com/>

The Ecologist

An environmental magazine founded in 1970, but relaunched online in 2009. It includes in-depth analysis alongside advice and news from around the world, as well as helpful book reviews.
<http://www.theecologist.org/>

Ecotextile News

Available by subscription, the Ecotextile News magazine provides the industry with the latest news and research, and is available in both online and offline formats.
<http://www.ecotextile.com/>

Ecouterre

A website aimed at the industry and consumers, which is dedicated to sustainable fashion and showcasing new designers.
<http://www.ecouterre.com/>

Inhabitat

A weblog for sustainable design, including fashion, which began in 2005. A good source of a wide range of design innovations and new ideas.
<http://inhabitat.com/tag/sustainable-fashion/>

Social Alterations

A UK-based interdisciplinary design website that is intended to support fashion design education by bringing together theory and practice. It focuses on social responsibility.
<http://socialalterations.com>

Treehugger

An international online sustainable magazine that includes a stream of sustainable fashion features, stories and articles.
<http://www.treehugger.com/>

Research centres and projects

Centre for Sustainable Fashion (CSF)

Based at the London College of Fashion, the CSF connects education, research and industry. The website links to research projects, reports and events, and the MA Fashion and The Environment course.
<http://www.sustainable-fashion.com/the-bulletin/>

Designing with People

Introduces 20 methods that can help designers engage with people during the design process.
<http://designingwithpeople.rca.ac.uk/methods>

IDEO HCD Toolkit

A US-based design company that has established a set of tools to help designers engage with approaches to human-centred design.
<http://www.hcdconnect.org/methods>

Inclusive Design Toolkit

A resource to help you engage with inclusive design. Provides an excellent tool for understanding how to assess the capabilities of users.
<http://www.inclusivedesign toolkit.com/betterdesign2/>

Textile Toolbox

Funded by the Swedish MISTRA organization, this is an initiative from TED at the Chelsea College of Art and Design. The site is a platform for fashion designers and experts to engage with new ideas. Contains interesting feature articles.
<http://www.textiletoolbox. com>

Tools and calculators

Carbon Calculator (UK)

An accessible and informative tool that enables you to measure and reduce your daily carbon footprint.
<http://carboncalculator. direct.gov.uk/index.html>

Carbon Trust (UK)

Provides a variety of free carbon footprint tools and resources for use within the workplace.
<http://www.carbontrust. com/resources>

EcoMetrics™

An online calculator designed to measure the environmental impacts of different textiles and processes.

The Higg Index

Developed by a group of industry partners, The Higg Index is a tool that enables you to measure the environmental and social performance of garments and footwear. You can download the index for use.
<http://www. apparelcoalition.org/ higgindex/>

Historic Futures

An online platform that enables producers and retailers to manage the traceability of their supply chain.
<https://www. stringtogether.com/>

United States Environmental Protection Agency

An Informative website that explains the issues concerned with greenhouse gas emissions and allows you to estimate your own footprint.
<http://www.epa.gov/ climatechange/ ghgemissions/>

Supporting organizations and advisory groups

UK

Environmental Justice Foundation

A non-profit organization that campaigns to protect the environment and defend human rights around the world. The website includes many films that drive home powerful messages. You can also support their work through the EJF shop.
<http://www.ejfoundation.org/>

Ethical Fashion Forum

Although UK-based, the network is international. The website provides a wide range of resources for designers and producers, and if you become a member you can attend webinars and other events.
<http://www.ethicalfashionforum.com/>

Labour Behind the Label

Campaign to improve conditions for workers in the clothing industry. The site provides access to a wide variety of educational resources. They are part of the international Clean Clothes Alliance.
<http://www.labourbehindthelabel.org/>

ASIA

Redress

A Hong Kong-based non-governmental organization that aims to promote sustainability in fashion within Asia. A good range of resources can be found on the website. Pays particular attention to reducing fabric waste, either during manufacture or at a garment's end-of-life.
<http://redress.com.hk/>

AUSTRALIA

Ethical Clothing Australia

Works with the local textile and fashion industry to ensure that Australian workers receive fair wages and decent conditions. Is particularly helpful with meeting Australian compliance laws and regulations.
<http://www.ethicalclothingaustralia.org.au/home/home>

EUROPE

Clean Clothes Campaign

An alliance of non-governmental organizations and trade unions, from 15 European states, although it also works with organizations in the USA, Australia and Canada. Covers a wide range of issues from women's rights and consumer advocacy to poverty reduction.
<http://www.cleanclothes.org/>

Fair Wear Foundation

An independent non-profit organization based in Amsterdam, but working internationally. Provides advice and support to industry to improve labour conditions for garment workers. Good, accessible resources are available on the website.
<http://www.fairwear.org/home/>

USA

Clean by Design, Natural Resources Defense Council

Aims to reduce the environmental impacts in manufacturing that are created by companies outsourced overseas. The website contains a wide range of reports and fact sheets about the impacts of manufacturing.
<http://www.nrdc.org/international/cleanbydesign/>

Fair Labor Association

The FLA is made up of universities, companies and organizations and aims to protect workers' rights around the world. It offers tools and resources to industry, and although based in the USA it has other international offices.
<http://www.fairlabor.org/>

Certification labels, legislation and support

Fairtrade International
From their headquarters in Germany and with associations around the world, FLO works with many organizations to set international FAIRTRADE standards and support fair trade producers.
<http://www.fairtrade.net/>

Global Organic Textile Standard (GOTS)
Made up of four member organizations from around the world, including the UK's Soil Association, the GOTS certification scheme ensures that a product contains at least 70% organic fibre.
<http://www.global-standard.org/>

Global Recycle Standard
Provides a certification mark for suppliers that produce fabric containing a set standard recycled content.
<http://textileexchange.org/content/global-recycle-standard>

MADE-BY
A not-for-profit European organization that supports labels and companies to make improvements across the life cycle of a garment. Partner companies can use the Made-By 'Blue Button' logo in garments and on swing tags as a way of visibly communicating their commitment.
<http://www.made-by.nl>

Oeko-Tex Standard 100 (EU)
An independent testing and certification body for textile materials and intermediate and final products. The label indicates that materials meet set standards and are harmless to health.
<https://www.oeko-tex.com/en/manufacturers/manufacturers.xhtml>

The Soil Association (UK)
A charity that works to promote healthy, humane and sustainable food, farming and land use. It is the UK's largest organic certification body, and includes organic textiles.
<http://www.soilassociation.org/>

World Fair Trade Organization
An international organization that operates in 75 countries and supports farmers, artisans and small producers by setting standards for fair trade business structures and practices. The WTFO logo is used by brands that meet their set standards.
<http://www.wfto.com/>

Sustainable fashion events, shows and competitions

EcoChic Design Award

Organized by the Redress organization in Asia, the competition accepts applications from graduates with fewer than three years' professional experience based in one of the identified countries. The brief focuses on reducing textile waste by designing mainstream fashion using one of three approaches – zero-waste, upcycling or reconstruction.
<http://www.ecochicdesignaward.com/>

Estethica, British Fashion Council

Founded by the BFC in 2006, the event, held during London Fashion Week, showcases ethical fashion from designers that meet set criteria. New designers can apply.
<http://www.britishfashioncouncil.co.uk/content/1146/Estethica>

RSA Student Design Awards

A long-running competition that briefs students to develop new ideas for contemporary problems. The brief's criteria involve, among other factors, providing social and/or environmental benefits. It is open to UK and international applicants who are enrolled on a course or are within one year of graduating.
<http://www.thersa.org/sda/home>

Sustainable Design Award, Ecco Domani Fashion Foundation Award

Offers funding to support US-based designers with fewer than five years' experience and at least one retail account to show at New York Fashion Week. Designers must demonstrate an awareness of environmental, social and economic issues.
<http://www.eccodomani.com/fashion-foundation/>

Fabrics, advice and support

C.L.A.S.S. (Creativity, Lifestyle and Sustainable Synergy)

Showrooms in Milan, London, Helsinki and Madrid each host an eco-materials library.
<http://www.classecohub.org/>

Copenhagen International Fashion Fair – Future Fabrics Fair and Conference

Held in Copenhagen for the fashion and furniture industries, the conference showcases new sustainable fabrics, fibres, trimmings and yarn.
<http://ciff.dk/>

Materia

Materia offers a free materials index and a searchable material database that presents detailed technical information in a user-friendly format.
<www.materia.nl>

Material ConneXion

An international consultancy and materials library. Based in more than ten countries, Material ConneXion provides a range of resource including material reports, and a library and online database accessible through university and school subscriptions.
<http://www.materialconnexion.com/Default.aspx>

The Sustainable Angle

A UK-based, not-for-profit organization that provides designers and manufacturers with help sourcing eco and sustainable fabrics and fibres. Outside the showroom, it presents its materials library at various events, such as the Future Fabrics Expo.
<http://www.thesustainableangle.org/>

Worn Again

Works with larger manufacturers to see the value in textile waste. The organization focuses on zero-waste, upcycling, downcycling, reuse and closed-loop systems.
<http://www.wornagain.co.uk/>

Allwood, J.M., Laursen, S.E., Maldivo de Rodriguez, C. and Bocken, N.M.P. (2006) *Well Dressed? The Present and Future Sustainability of Clothing and Textiles in the United Kingdom.* Cambridge: Institute for Manufacturing, University of Cambridge.

Black, S. (2008) *Eco-Chic: The Fashion Paradox.* London: Black Dog Publishing.

Black, S. (2012) *The Sustainable Fashion Handbook.* London: Thames & Hudson.

Bras-Klapwijk, R.M. and Knot, J.M.C. (2001) *Strategic Environmental Assessment for Sustainable Households in 2050: illustrated for clothing.* Journal of Sustainable Development, 9(2), 109–118.

Carson, R. (2000) *Silent Spring (new ed).* Penguin Books. London: Penguin Books.

Chapman, J. (2005) *Emotionally Durable Design: Objects, Experience and Empathy.* London: Earthscan.

Crul, M. and Diehl, J.C. (2006) *Design for Sustainability: A Practical Approach For Developing Economies.* [Online] Paris: United Nations Environment Program/DELFT University of Technology. Available: <http://www.d4s-de.org/manual/d4stotalmanual.pdf> *[accessed 10.12.2009].*

Datschefski, E. (2001) *The Total Beauty of Sustainable Products.* Crans-Pres-Celigny: Rotovision.

Diviney, E. and Lillywhite, S. (2009) *Travelling Textiles: A Sustainability Roadmap of Natural Fibre Garments.* [Online] Melbourne: Brotherhood of St Laurence. Available: <http://thehub.ethics.org.au/sme/sector_product_roadmaps> [accessed 5.6.2010].

Draper, S., Murray, V. and Weissbrod, I. (2007) *Fashioning Sustainability: A Review of the Sustainability Impacts of the Clothing Industry.* [Online] London: Forum for the Future. Available: <www.forumforthefuture.org.uk> [accessed 3.9.2007].

Fisher, T., Cooper, T., Woodward, S., Hiller, A. and Gorowek, H. (2008) *Public Understanding of Sustainable Clothing: A Report for the Department for Environment, Food and Rural Affairs.* [Online] London: DEFRA. Available: <http://randd.defra.gov.uk/Default.aspx?Menu=Menu&Module=More&Location=None&Completed=0&ProjectID=15626> [accessed 15.6.2009].

Fletcher, K. (2008) *Sustainable Fashion and Textiles: Design Journeys.* London: Earthscan.

Fletcher, K. & Grose, L. (2012) *Fashion and Sustainability: Design for Change.* London: Laurence King.

Fuad-Luke, A. (2002) *The Eco-Design Handbook.* London: Thames & Hudson.

Fuad-Luke, A. (2009) *Design Activism: Beautiful Strangeness for a Sustainable World.* London: Earthscan.

Gwilt, A. and Rissanen, T. (eds.) (2011) *Shaping Sustainable Fashion.* London: Earthscan.

Hart, A. and North, S. (1998) *Historical Fashion in Detail: The 17th and 18th Centuries.* London: V&A Publishing.

Hethorn, J. and Ulasewicz, C. (eds.) (2008) *Sustainable Fashion: Why Now? A Conversation About Issues, Practices, and Possibilities.* New York: Fairchild Books.

Jenkyn-Jones, S. (2002) *Fashion Design*. London: Laurence King Publishing.

Manzini, E. and Jégou, F. (eds.) 2003. *Sustainable Everyday: Scenarios of Urban Life*. Milan: Edizioni Ambiente.

McDonough, W. and Braungart, M. (2002) *Cradle to Cradle: Remaking the Way we Make Things*. New York: North Point Press.

O'Mahony, M. (2012) *Advanced Textiles for Health and Wellbeing*. London: Thames & Hudson.

Palmer, A. (2001) *Couture and Commerce: The Transatlantic Fashion Trade in the 1950s*. Toronto: UBC Press.

Papanek, V. (1995) *The Green Imperative: Ecology and Ethics in Design and Architecture*. London: Thames & Hudson.

Renfrew, E. and Renfrew, C. (2009) *Basics Fashion Design: Developing a Collection*. Lausanne: AVA Publishing.

Sanders, A. and Seager, K. (2009) *Junky Styling: Wardrobe Surgery*. London: A&C Black.

Seivewright, S. (2012) *Basics Fashion Design: Research and Design*. Lausanne: AVA Publishing.

Shaeffer, C.B. (1993) *Couture Sewing Techniques*. Newtown: Taunton Press.

Shove, E. (2003) *Comfort, Cleanliness and Convenience*. Oxford: Berg.

Sinha, P. (2000) *The Role of Design Through Making Across Market Levels in the UK Fashion Industry*. Design Journal, 3(3), 26–44.

Sorger, R. and Udale, J. (2012) The Fundamentals of Fashion Design (2nd ed). Lausanne: AVA Publishing.

Stecker, P. (1996) *Fashion Design Manual*. Melbourne: Macmillan Education Australia.

Thorpe, A. (2007) *The Designer's Atlas of Sustainability*. Washington: Island Press.

Troy, N.J. (2003) *Couture Cultures: A Study of Modern Art and Fashion*. Cambridge, MA: MIT Press.

Vezzoli, C. and Manzini, E. (2008) *Design for Environmental Sustainability*. London: Springer.

Wilcox, C. (2007) *The Golden Age of Couture*. London: V & A Publishing.

Acknowledgements

I would like to warmly thank all of the students, graduates, designers and fashion labels that have contributed to this book. In particular, I wish to thank the following people for their assistance:

Claire Bergkamp at Stella McCartney; Annika Matilda Wendelboe; Susan Dimasi; Isabell de Hillerin; Lizzie Harrison; Wayne Hemingway; Rebecca Atherton at Antiform; Christina Dean, Sofia Tarnberg and Hannah Lane at ReDress; David Telfer; Arne Eberle PR; and Vibeke Riisberg and Kjetil Aas at Kolding School of Design.

Thank you also to the Ethical Fashion Forum network and its members for their contributions. Although we could not feature everyone, it is pleasing to see so much good work happening.

Also, I would like to thank everyone at Fairchild Books, including Georgia Kennedy and Helen Stallion. In particular, I have to thank Lynsey Brough, my editor, for her advice, support and ongoing enthusiasm for this book.

Finally, I would like to thank Ian and Dylan for their continual love, support and patience.

Picture credits

p007 Image by Stelianour Sani, designed and made by Emma Rees for REtrose; pp008–9 Courtesy of Iñiy Sanchez; p011 Image by Will Whipple; p014-15 Courtesy of Forum for the Future; p016 Courtesy of M&S; p017 Courtesy of Kate Fletcher; p018 Courtesy of Edun; p021 Patagonia © 2013 Patagonia Inc.; p022 © Alice Payne, 2011; p023 Courtesy of Junky Styling, image by Michael Heilgemeir; p024 Courtesy of People Tree; p025 Images by Kyle Ross; p026 Courtesy of the Environmental Justice Foundation (EJF); p027 Image by Alex Sturrock; p029 Courtesy of Matilda Wendelboe; p031 Copyright Speedo International Limited; p033 Courtesy of Clara Vuletich, images by Robert Self; p035 All rights reserved © Gunas USA Inc.; p036 Courtesy of Gorman; p038 Image by Antti Ahtiluoto; p040 Image by Candace Meyer; p041 [2.11] Katherine Neumann/House of Wandering Silk; [2.13] Courtesy of Kallio NYC; p042 Courtesy of Martina Spetlova; p044–45 [2.15–2.21] Courtesy of Stefanie Nieuwenhuyse; [2.22] Image by James Champion; p047 Courtesy of Stella McCartney; p48 Courtesy of Mirozlav Zaruba (Photographer for Tammam); p051 Courtesy of Lilia Yip (designer), Marina de Magalhaes (stylist), Mariell Amelie (photographer), Adlena Dignam (hair), Michelle Dacillio (make-up); p052 [3.2] Design by Anna Ruohonen, image by Victor Matussiere; [3.3] Image by Canghai (model: Lan Zhang); p053 Courtesy of Lilia Yipp (design), Jessica Kneipp (photographer), Haruka Abe (model); p054 © Cherelle Abrams; p055 © Alice Payne, 2012; p057 [3.8 and 3.9] © Mark Rogers, Pachacuti; [3.10] Courtesy of Beate Godager (design and styling), Amanda Hestehave (photography), Tina Kristofferson (make-up), Julie Hasselby (model); p058 Courtesy of Tara Baoth Mooney; p059 Courtesy of Eunjeong Jeon; p060 © Gorunway; p061 © Amy Ward, sustainable designer; p062–63 [3.16] Image by Marek Neuman; [3.17 and 3.18] Courtesy of Alabama Chanin, image by Robert Rausch; p064 [3.19] Courtesy of Julika Works; [3.20] Courtesy of C.L.A.S.S; p067 [3.22] © Ainokainen, image by Kai Lindqvist; [3.23 and 3.24] Courtesy of Refinity with Anne Noor degraaf, More Tea Vicar, Janneke Tol (photographer), and Lori Schriekenberg (model); p068–9 [3.25–9] © Dr Kate Goldsworthy; [3.30] ©Hiroshi Sugimoto, Stylized Sculpture 026,2007, Tao Kurihara, 2007 (Dress: Collection of the Kyoto Costume Institute); p070–3 Courtesy of Annika Matilda Wendelboe; p074 Courtesy of Chloe Mukai/ITC; p076 © David Telfer; p077 © Titania Inglis, image by Evan Browning; p078 © Elementum by Daniela Pais, image by Anabel Luna; p079 [4.7 and 4.8] Courtesy of the Science Museum/Science & Society Picture Library; p081 [4.11] Courtesy of Haider Ackermann (top design), Fiona Mills (trouser design), image by Nail Yang; [4.12] Courtesy of V&A Images; p082–3 Courtesy of Line Sander Johansen; p084–5 Image by Hiroshi Iwasaki ©Miyake Design Studio; p086 [4.22] © Howies; [4.23] © Rad Hourani Inc.; p087 Design by Allenomis, image by Sonihairle MacDonald; model Caeley Elcock (ColourAgency); p088–9 © Naomi Bailey-Cooper; p091 [4.27] ©Marimekko; [4.28] Courtesy of Getty; p092-93 [4.30] Courtesy of Getty; [3.29, 4.31-2] Courtesy of MATERIALBYPRODUCT; p095 © Shamila at Eric Elenaas Agency; p096-97 © Suno; p098 © Kate Holt; p100 © everlasting sprout; p101 Image by Sally Cole Photography; p102-3 Courtesy of Awamaki, images by Kate Reeder <www.katereeder.com>; p104-7 [5.11] © Xavier Busch; [5.12-5.16] © Photography by Amos Fricke, styling by Anja Niedermeir, hair and make-up by Sarah Marx, model Liuba (Iconic Management); p108–9 Courtesy of Continuum; p110 [5.19] © SANS Atelier LLC; [5.20]Image by Rosie Martin, model Angel Hook; p111 © Courtesy of Anatomy Vintage and Etsy; p113 Courtesy of Daijiro Mizuno; p114 Courtesy of Xeni; p117 Courtesy of Emma Dulcie Rigby, image by Sean Michael; p118 Courtesy of Ecover; p121 [6.3] Courtesy of Emma Dulcie Rigby, image by Sean Michael; p121 Courtesy of Oxfam; p122 Courtesy of V&A Images; p123 Design by Sukiennik Agnieszka; p125 [6.8] Refinity with Berber Soepboer, image by Savale; [6.9] Courtesy of Bruno Kleist <www.brunokleist.com>, image by Michael Nguyen; p126 Courtesy of Heleen Klopper, image by Mandy Pieper; p127 © Sara McBeen; p128 Images by Emanuel Brás; p129 © Lisa Hawthorn, 2011; p131 Courtesy of V&A Images; p132-3 © Bob and John Knitwear 2012; p134-7 Courtesy of Lizzie Harrison; p139 Courtesy of ETPTT Martin Ueberschaer (photographer), Ellen E/ Modelfabrik (model), Bianca Bensch (make-up/hair); p140 Image by Alfredo Salazer; p141 [7.3] Courtesy of Esther Lui Po Chu; [7.4] Courtesy of Katherine Gram Hvejsel (designer) and Anders Fuerby (photographer); p142 Courtesy of Remade in Switzerland, image by Yann Gross; p143 Courtesy of Wister Tsang; p144 © Queenie and Ted; p145 Courtesy of the author; p146 ©Camilla Greenwell; p147 [7.14 and 7.15] Design by Jennifer Whitty and Holly McQuillan, images by Thomas McQuillan, model Monica Buchan-Ng, styling by Jennifer Whitty, assisted by Alex Barton, photography post-production by Holly McQuillan; [7.18] Courtesy of Martina Spetlova; p148-9 © Till Bovermann; p150 Courtesy of Carmen Atigas; p151 Courtesy of Zegna; p152-3 [7.22 and 7.23] Courtesy of Katie Ledger; [7.24] © Teijin; p154 Courtesy of Eva Aude, Ramona Reile, Petja Zorec, Vibe Lindhardt Fællend; p155 Courtesy of Dr Kate Goldsworthy; p156–7 Courtesy of Hemingway Design; p159 Image by Canghai; model: Lan Zhang.